# Saving Union Station

# SAVING UNION STATION

## An Inside Look at Historic Preservation

By Thomas Finnegan

WASHINGTON PARK PRESS LTD.
Albany, New York

Special Commemorative Printing, August 1989
Manufactured in the United States of America
93  92  91  90  89  5  4  3  2

Published by Washington Park Press Ltd.
7 Englewood Place
Albany, New York 12203

Library of Congress Cataloging-in-Publication Data

Finnegan, Thomas, 1947–
Saving Union Station: an inside look at historic preservation /
    Thomas Finnegan.
    Includes index.
    ISBN 0-9605460-8-1.   ISBN 0-9605460-7-3 (pbk.)
    1. Union Station (Albany, N.Y.) — Conservation and restoration.
2. Albany (N.Y.) — Buildings, structures, etc. — Conservation and
restoration.  I. Title.
NA6313.A43F5    1988    725'.31'02880974 — dc19    88-17390

For Joyce and Donna

Peter D. Kiernan.

# Prologue, Epilogue, Eulogy

Peter D. Kiernan relished challenges. He delighted in applying wits, strength, and will to the quest for elegant solutions. Fear of failure never daunted him. So in January 1984, when the seemingly outrageous idea of converting Union Station into corporate headquarters for Norstar Bancorp flashed before him, he confidently followed his intuition.

Of course, it was easy, gazing at the sullied yet once splendid train station, to romanticize the idea of renovation. But there were innumerable obstacles to realizing the dream: regulatory approvals, engineering difficulties, fragile morale . . . and cost, the greatest uncertainty of all. What was the idea worth? What would be the return on the investment? Would the public (especially customers and shareholders) criticize the expenditure, or deride the project's final form? The challenge was not just Peter's. There were many other people involved — to whom he was accountable.

His intuition assured him he was right to try. Once committed, he relied on his greatest talent: motivating people. He engendered intense enthusiasm as he imparted his vision to employees, architects, designers, planners, engineers, preservationists, civic officials, the media. Soon they, too, were certain the project would succeed. Some had to shoulder heavy workloads and pressing deadlines, but in that measure they shared the glory of achievement.

Peter Kiernan knew the deepest secret in the art of leadership: that each participant celebrates *personal* triumph over challenge. The final pride belongs to every man and woman involved. Proof of that was in countless faces at the inaugural festivities.

In August 1988, as this book neared completion, Peter Kiernan was stricken, having savored the pleasures of his splendid office at the southeast corner of Norstar Plaza for less than two years. His funeral was on September 19, 1988 — two years to the day after the grand opening of the building which will always remain, in the public mind, "his."

He would *never,* in his lifetime, have allowed his name to be affixed to this landmark; it was to be a monument not to himself but rather to corporate esprit, craftsmanship, and community pride. But one year after his passing, there should be no hesitation in allowing a new name, Peter D. Kiernan Plaza, to adorn an inspired idea parlayed into proud accomplishment.

# Contents

# Preface

You read or hear that a grand old building downtown is going to be saved. Two years later, you read or hear about the big opening celebration of the spectacularly renovated grand old building downtown. These news stories, brief intrusions into daily preoccupations, give you momentary joy (it's right that fine architecture should be preserved — especially where you might see it now and then while driving by). Then you return to more pressing matters.

Unless you have devoted sweat and love to the rehab project or the campaign to return it to life, you may have little idea of what is involved. What happens inside an historic renovation project, behind plywood parapets? Do they just gut the place and repaint? How much can they gut? What if they gut too much? How do they retain ornamental splendor, and architectural integrity, if they gut a place? Who's *they*?

The questions are countless, even in seemingly simple matters. Should the owner restore the original colors? What if they've been lost through decades of neglect? What if the new owner likes dark purple? Does it matter if customers, employees, the local media, the mayor, the architects and designers, government regulators and officials *don't* like dark purple? What say do they have in the owner's choice of colors — and why should all of this matter anyway?

Dark purple may be an extreme instance. Rearranging the interior of an historic building is a more frequent proposal. What if you, the new owner, would like to turn the place upside down, in effect? Who would object, why, and to what avail? "It's my money," you might say; "shouldn't I have my way?"

The answer seems clear: it would be your building, all right, but not your neighborhood, your downtown, your community (whether in a zoning or a spiritual sense). There is a deeper issue here.

Today's historic-preservation movement enjoys momentum and universal approbation. But that success is recent and hard-won. To look at one major *adaptive-use historic renovation* (and each word in that long phrase is weighty) is to see both the past and the present state of our societal perspective on the saving of old buildings.

I hope that the immediacy and clear focus of a single case study will give insight into the complex task of saving historical and architectural landmarks which cannot be duplicated. But keep in mind that although the Union Station story centers on a building, it's a story of people. We can focus here on only a few of the hundreds of men and women who lovingly revived Union Station. As you read, reflect on what this project meant to each one. They cared about what they were doing; they will be pleased by your awakened appreciation.

From its inception, Union Station was built by and for people like you and me. Nearly obliterated, it's still with us. I hope that an illuminating look will help you enjoy it to the fullest.

# Acknowledgments

If only a few of the hundreds of players in the Union Station story can be introduced by name, fewer still can be thanked personally in this limited space. And thanks are also due to many people who were not there in Norstar Plaza but who have contributed eagerly to this book. Let this be a heartfelt, though necessarily incomplete, paean of gratitude.

The principals of the story — Peter Kiernan, Steven Einhorn, Julie Stokes, Bob Sweeney (now a valued friend), and Ben Soep — were generous with precious time and forthright comment. Tom Birdsey, Len Fox, Ron Noll, and Ed Grey never said no to a request for information. Joyce Flanagan, whose work transcends job description, was in effect my secretary without ever having suspected it. Special thanks go to John Myers, who went far beyond any conceivable sense of duty in giving me time and help. And here's my expression of supreme gratitude to Bob Sloan, now retired from Fleet/Norstar, who surpassed even these eager contributors and volunteered to scrutinize the entire manuscript to aid my effort at a balanced perspective.

The outside insiders? The librarians, historians, collectors, railroad enthusiasts, photographers, researchers, and others who happily played a role (in this and many other projects in my work with Norstar) for which they never expected any recognition. That includes Chris Robinson, Chris Beauregard, Jan Johnstone, Jim Hobin, Tim Truscott, Roni Evangelista, Doug Barron, Morris Gerber, Don Barbeau, Harvey Vlahos (who shaped a creative vision of Norstar Plaza in another medium), and my superb administrative assistant, Nelly Mitchell. Neither should anonymity claim a talented photographer, Donna Abbott, who took the bulk of the photographs which Norstar has graciously allowed me to use. Two other outsiders who were once insiders also deserve thanks for having extended to me such an opportunity as this: Donna Brennan and Barry Brandt.

At Washington Park Press, Susanne Dumbleton is to manuscripts what the star players mentioned above are to building renovation. Wordsmithing aside, Anne Older has proved no less capable with every other aspect of book publishing. It's been a revelation, most exhilarating, and ultimately wholly rewarding.

I haven't forgotten Chris, a terrific wife and an even better manager.

# The Background

Exactly twenty-five years before this story took its jubilant turn toward a happy ending, the editor of *Trains* magazine devoted the April 1959 issue to a careful analysis of the crisis in America's passenger railroad service. To look at the serious problem of large downtown terminal buildings accommodating dwindling ridership, David P. Morgan had his staff illustrate a possible solution by using a fictitious but exemplary "Union Station," an "old 1900-era structure, inspired by an actual building."

There, laid out on the editorial operating table, cleverly flipped end-over-end but nevertheless quite recognizable, was Albany's own Union Station. Morgan's thoughtful prescription: complete bypass.

"The problem is resolved," Morgan began, ". . . by moving the station site to a location . . . much nearer the residential area of the city." Parking would be much improved at the new site across the river, he said, since, "being pre-automobile in origin, the [present] station is inconveniently planted in downtown traffic congestion." The new station "is attractive but small, hence less expensive to build, heat, light and maintain, and easier for passengers to use." Along with the drawings of "OLD Union Station" and its successor, Morgan presented a track plan which "eliminates a downtown passenger-only railroad line, thus clearing some valuable real estate for development and boosting utilization of remaining trackage."

We must realize that editor Morgan was addressing a railroading audience and that it was the age of the national interstate highway system and urban renewal — that night of the bulldozers which preceded the dawn of historic preservationism (Penn Station in New York City would be demolished the following year). Thus Morgan and the station planners showed little concern about what would become of "the old 1900-era structure."

"Look again," the article urged. "Wouldn't this work in *your* city, too?"

---

The management of the New York Central thought so. As early as 1955, the railroad had been considering abandoning downtown passenger depots; on August 20, 1956, the company announced plans to close 406 passenger stations, including the Union Stations in Albany and neighboring Schenectady. "Excess and obsolete property," they were called. Yet even as these plans advanced, the public timetables still cheerily proclaimed advantageous service: "When you take to the high road aboard a sleek New York Central streamliner, your traveling begins and ends right in the heart of town — *at a convenient downtown terminal.*"

In Albany there were people intent on "clearing some valuable real estate for development." Mayor Erastus Corning II, on the other hand, knew that closing Union Station would effectively shut down the heart of town. While New York Central President Alfred E. Perlman professed to journalists his concern for urban redevelopment, Corning's city administration mobilized to keep station-stop "Albany" from moving to Rensselaer (that new location proposed in the *Trains* piece). A bitter confrontation was inevitable. Hearkening back to Revolutionary times, people joked about "drums along the Hudson."

---

In 1818, the United States of America was a small nation, its twelve million people still anchored to the East Coast. To the north and west, Maine and Michigan were wilderness territories, not yet states. When Illinois acquired statehood that year, the population of Chicago was not even six thousand.

Albany, New York, though, was a leading city in the young seaboard nation. The great Appalachian mountain range, stretching from Canada to Alabama, effectively separated the exclamation point of the bustling seacoast from the question mark of the wild interior. When people headed for the limitless middle western lands, it was via the Great Inland Lakes and the Mississippi River, not over the mountains. There were only three feasible places to develop true mountain crossings, and it was Albany's good fortune to be on the best of the three. Unlike the Wilderness Road at the junction of the borders of Kentucky, Virginia, and Tennessee, and the National Road across Maryland, the Great Genesee Road's Mohawk Turnpike followed a water-level route.

Those "Roads" were actually trails, sometimes the width of a single horse, and of course they were vulnerable to mud and snow. The water-level Mohawk Turnpike, too, was often more wilderness path than comfortable conveyance. Water routes had long been preferred (freight could be shipped from Europe more economically than it could be moved 30 miles inland), but the Mohawk River was turbulent and long-freezing, dangerous when high and impassable when low.

The idea of a great canal was irresistible, although in 1818 the engineering obstacles were formidable. A "Big Ditch" from Albany to Buffalo would require 363 miles of excavation with shovels and wheelbarrows. The canal would have to be carried *over* rivers, valleys, and city streets, with every vertical foot hard-earned and costly. From the time the New York State Bank of Albany bought the first bonds in 1817, the outcome was dubious and hotly debated. Yet the engineering miracle was achieved, and from its opening in 1825, the Erie Canal proved immensely profitable. The Great Lakes and the Midwest could now be reached comfortably from New York in only four days. At Albany travelers and freight switched between Erie Canal packet boats and Hudson River steamers. The capital city of the Empire State flourished.

Yet there were real problems. In the long winters the canal and the Hudson froze. The level route was not a direct route. Just 17 linear miles separated Schenectady on the Mohawk from Albany on the Hudson, but the canal required a stair of locks, a 40-mile course, and several hours' travel between the two cities.

It took a visionary like George Featherstonhaugh, an avid reader on the latest experiments with steam machines and "rail roads" in Great Britain, to reappraise what seemed perfectly good transportation. Just as the "Big Ditch" in 1818 had seemed sheer folly, so too did a functioning railroad open to the public only a few years later. Steam locomotion in 1825 was hardly less experimental than fusion is today; the earliest U.S. railroads, such as the Baltimore & Ohio, planned to use horses as motive power. What we think of as heavy steel rail was then a mere flat strip nailed to wooden beams, quickly crushed by the first locomotives. More tellingly, one railroad had to hire Daniel Webster to counter the persistent rumor that rail travel would lead to brain damage. People wanted proof that as they hurtled 20 miles in an hour human blood would not boil. Even as the earliest trains lurched into action, there were still troubles. Following the explosion of its first locomotive, a southern railroad publicized use of a barrier wagon, loaded with cotton bales, between engine and cars: "It will protect travelers when [not "if"!] the locomotive explodes."

Featherstonhaugh found the wealthy and influential backing he needed in Albany's richest citizen, Stephen Van Rensselaer, and obtained the first known railroad charter in the U.S. in April 1826. The two were careful to suggest that their line would run only *between* the Mohawk and Hudson rivers, so as not to enrage the powerful and protectionist canal interests. Once again the State Bank of Albany stepped up and offered to finance the purchase of the right-of-way.

The celebrated opening of the Mohawk & Hudson Railroad, on August 9, 1831, effectively began regular passenger railroad transportation in America. What a maiden run it was! The locomotive (named after De Witt Clinton, the political force behind the Erie Canal), the size of a subcompact car and far less powerful, without bell, whistle, or brakes, jerked its three Albany-built, flange-wheeled stage coaches into motion, set fire to clothing and then to hastily-raised parasols with its shower of wood-fuel sparks, terrified spectators' horses and upset buggies, and wobbled off

at up to 30 miles per hour for Schenectady, banging the cars together at the first water stop, where a better form of coupling was improvised and they were off again!

The next day the Mohawk & Hudson started regular passenger operation. A ticket for the 45-minute trip was 50 cents. The railroad joined the Erie Canal at both termini, where stationary steam engines raised and lowered the passenger cars by cable between rail and water line. An harmonious coupling of technologies now moved travelers efficiently, though not exactly in comfort, on their journeys from New York to Albany and the West.

As all of America wondered at such accomplishment, improvements came rapidly and the line prospered. Albany's Mohawk & Hudson quickly became the first commercially successful passenger railroad in the U.S. Across New York State small lines sprang up between every pair of important or self-important towns. Gentlemen's coffeehouses served as incubators for start-up railroad ventures. But the climate was also right for con artists and speculators. Fraud and bribery were rampant. The current phrase, "as worthless as railroad stock," betrayed the reality of oversubscription, overbuilding, and overzealous management. The load on the nascent American economy was severe: the nation's first great economic crisis, the Panic of 1837, was definitely a consequence of railroad fever.

This was the rough-and-tumble context when in June 1853 two eminent Albanians, Erastus Corning, formerly of the self-same State Bank of Albany, and attorney John V. L. Pruyn, consolidated the string of small railroads between Albany and Buffalo into the New York Central Railroad. Truly a giant system in its day, and for a time the largest corporation in the United States, the Central could finally lay to rest many of the inconveniences of long-distance rail travel. Thanks to through connections and baggage-checking, plush new cars (on heavier rails), accommodations for female passengers, regulated fares for the cabs outside the stations, and niceties such as ice water in warm weather, rail passage from Albany to the west attained great popularity. Just two decades after the tumult of the "De Witt Clinton's" maiden run, life without trains was a fast-fading recollection.

The final link in the great chain would be direct rail service between New York City and Albany. But the engineering hurdles and political obstructions were formidable. Who else but a wealthy "Commodore" with a fleet of steamships could recognize the potential of an almost gradeless, efficient, water-level route from New York to Chicago, and then leverage the great task to completion?

Cornelius Vanderbilt had the cash and the cunning needed to merge the larger, uncooperative New York Central into his brand new, splendidly engineered railroad up the Hudson River. After several formal overtures were rebuffed, Vanderbilt (who already had sizable but noncontrolling interest in the Central) took a shrewd gamble. On January 17, 1867, he suddenly halted all connecting service to the Central outside Albany — forcing passengers out into a blizzard to cross the frozen Hudson on foot. The hardship produced the calculated effect — public outrage — and stock in the railroads involved dropped rapidly in anticipation of calamity. Three days later Vanderbilt informed a convulsed State Legislature that service was being fully resumed. Albany got the message: Vanderbilt had bought up what he needed in New York Central stock.

After Vanderbilt's death in 1877, true ownership in the New York Central was gradually dispersed among "a great brood of hungry little Vanderbilts of all sorts,"[1] and a line of career men ascended to control. Autocracy yielded to management. Industrial and financial America was moving beyond impetuous adolescence. A mature railroad industry, one less vulnerable to caprice and greed and more receptive to the needs and wishes of its customers, was evolving.

With consolidation came a crush of passenger traffic through Albany. In the decade 1890 to 1900, immigrant passenger traffic was breaking ridership records. From New York and Boston (the Central's de facto control of the Boston & Albany was legitimated in 1899 as a perpetual lease), through traffic to Chicago inundated the unassuming Albany Union Depot of 1872. Boston's South Station opened in 1898; it would remain for nearly twenty years the largest and busiest station in the country. The second of the Grand Centrals rose in New York. At the symbolic center of the immense New York Central & Hudson River Railroad system was Albany, still the site of the directors' annual meeting. For reasons of corporate image as well as function, then, a large new station should be erected in the capital of the Empire State.[2]

Erastus Corning: banker,
businessman, railroad president,
politician, and more.

The project would also involve extensive track, bridge, and traffic improvements, since Albany was the division point at the crossroads through which passed "the world's only four-track main line," as the Central proudly boasted. The city of Albany eagerly assisted by arranging to sell to the Central the property adjacent to the old Union Depot. That land was the site of the famous Delavan House, the hotel which had hosted President-elect Lincoln and countless people of celebrity, and which had long served as a makeshift seat of government for the politicians overcrowding the Old Capitol building. The grand hotel, in front of which the ceremonial first train of the New York Central had awaited its dignitaries back in June 1853, had burned tragically in 1894.

Amid the ashes of the capital's famous hotel, a million of its bricks, many still clumped in melted glass and lead, were salvaged to contribute to the New York Central's, and Albany's, new Union Station.

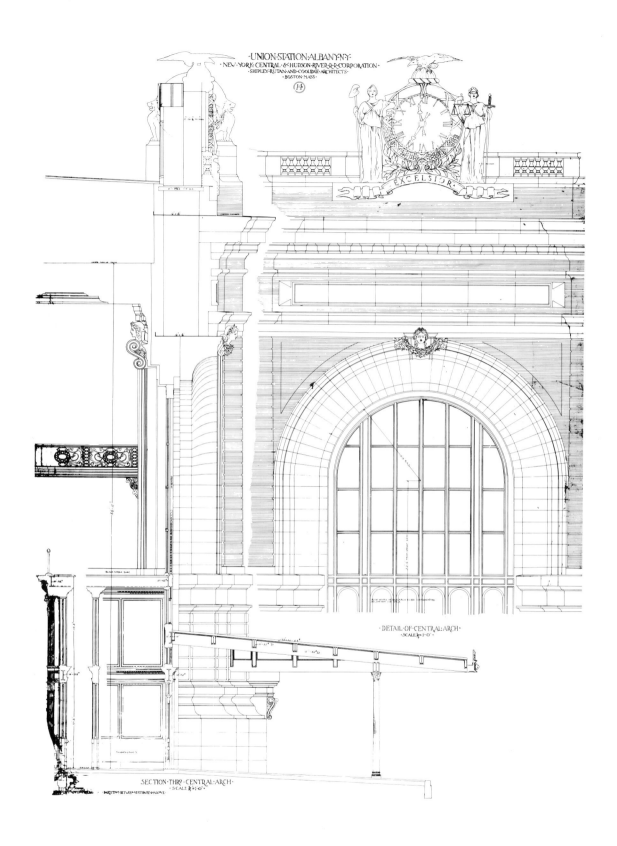

·UNION·STATION·ALBANY·N·Y·
NEW·YORK·CENTRAL·&·HUDSON·RIVER·R·R·CORPORATION
·SHEPLEY·RUTAN·AND·COOLIDGE·ARCHITECTS·
·BOSTON·MASS·

EXCELSIOR

·DETAIL·OF·CENTRAL·ARCH·
·SCALE ½"=1'-0'·

·SECTION·THR°·CENTRAL·ARCH·
·SCALE ¾"=1'-0'·

The handsome blueprints of
Shepley, Rutan, and Coolidge
reveal attention to detail
throughout.

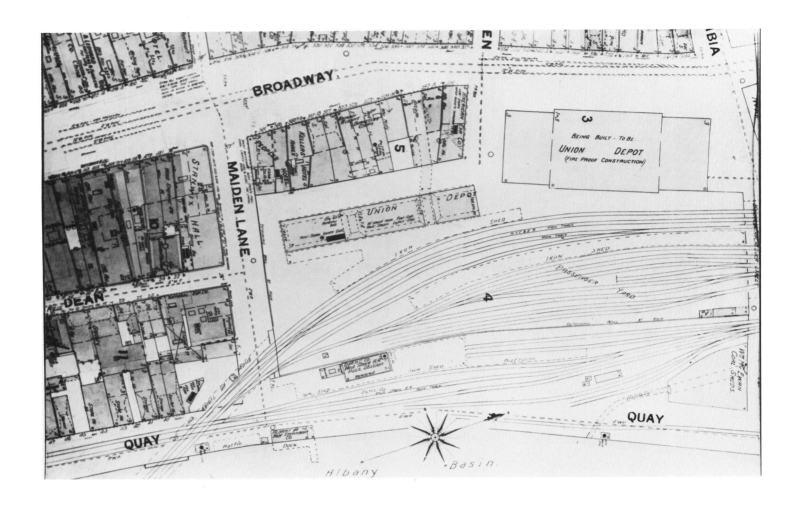

Map of 1898 shows the old
depot alongside the proposed
new station (on the site of the
Delavan House). Note the
arcade connecting the old
depot to Broadway.

# The Building

How can you, from your space-age vantage point, look at a turn-of-the-century railroad station and actually *see* it? You have to imagine.

Picture a sky without vapor trails. Picture buildings tall, yes, but not so tall you can't easily count the stories. Some buildings have elevators; some are "fireproofed." Most are built with simple derricks, but few machines — there is no high-speed this or high-pressure that. Picture streets where horses outnumber those comical, newfangled automobiles two thousand to one. Europe is ten days away. When travelers depart for Chicago (merely an overnight ride), there's no shriek of turbines, but rather a pure whistle and a whump of steam power.

Now take a deep breath. Put yourself *in* the age. You're a day laborer, recently arrived from the Continent. You're conscious of having a strong back and skilled hands; they're your livelihood in this new world. Now let out the breath. Relax. Yes, you work hard. But you know how to relax, too. You take walks along quiet, peopled boulevards. You look forward to a Sunday afternoon at home, with family chatter and an empty calendar. Movies? No, but there are photographs. They're even beginning to put photographs in the newspapers.

When you snap on an electric light, you still sometimes smile with satisfaction. Electric motors are becoming commonplace, even in the home; how much better life is sure to become! You've heard a gramophone and talked through a telephone (but you remain skeptical when people describe to you the "radio").

Pick up a paper (no photographs in this one). Read of a horrible accident, with upwards of *twenty* victims! Read of typhus on the rampage downstate . . . and then in the adjacent column read of a newly developed potion to combat catarrh (read that without recognizing it as a paid advertisement). Read curiously of a new product with the odd name of Jell-O, a packet of which carries the steep price of 15 cents. At your laborer's wages, that's an hour's work! Admire the drawing (no photos) of a fine pair of shoes, priced at "only" $4.00 . . . and realize that you would have to work *27 hours* to buy them. *Twenty-seven hours:* exactly three working days.

Then get dressed, select a suitable hat, bundle up, and walk to work. You work on the rising form of the new depot on Broadway, on the spot where the Delavan House Hotel burned down on December 30, 1894 . . . just about five years ago.

The new depot is an immense undertaking. Strong backs and simple shovels have excavated most of the cavernous foundations, down into the Delavan House rubble. Manual labor has wrestled the 15-ton granite blocks onto and off the big wooden derrick; the walls have been rising steadily. Out back new trackage, subterranean walkways, bridges, and platforms are taking shape (while the trains roll in and out, unimpeded). Only about ninety men are on the job now; in the summer it was over two hundred. They said in the papers back in June last year ('98) that the railroad "agrees to fully complete it within one year after

One of only three known photos
of Union Station under construction. Beneath a giant sign
("Norcross Brothers Builders")
trains continue using the old
depot (at left).

work is commenced." You smile. That's impossible. This is a giant building, and the workers are only humans, not machines, and the work's going to stop any day now for the Albany winter. They'll be lucky to open it by New Year's of 1901.

In the north wing, they're assembling an entire iron-work shop. They've brought in all the equipment to make cast-iron railings and galleries, right here on the spot! The ceiling is almost complete, over its riveted beams. The last stone, a chimney cap, is going up later today. You hear that the stone carvers, who will be producing the statues around the clock up on the front of the building, are going to earn something like 75 cents an hour. Now, what in the world have they got that you haven't got? You scratch your head, pick up your shovel, and get back to work.

Go forward now, a year exactly, to December 17, 1900. You're prying up the frosty sidewalk outside the new depot, working at 5:30 a.m. It's cold out here! But will you look at this crowd? The new depot is going to open any minute now. And you've decided, emboldened by a bit of liquor, that you're going to be the very first person to step through the door. You hear a carriage behind you, just as what's-his-name peeks out from inside the front door . . .

> At five-thirty o'clock this morning,

you read, chagrined, that evening in the Albany *Times-Union,*

> the doors of the new depot were thrown open to the public. Mr. Frank A. Harrington, superin-tendent of the Mohawk division, was the first

person to enter the officially unlocked doors. His carriage arrived at the front entrance at 5:30 o'clock, just as Louis Jeannin, the foreman for Norcross Bros., was unlocking the door. [Harrington] saw the act and with a quickened footstep defeated a pedestrian who was also striving for the honor. As Mr. Harrington passed in, Mr. Jeannin said, "Let me congratu-late you, Mr. Harrington, on being the first person to enter the unlocked doors of the depot." Mr. Harrington thanked him and then looked around with a smile of satisfaction.

You harrumph and slouch back into obscurity.

The opening, though unceremonious, has a festive feel. The newspaper reporter records all the details of the first ticket bought and the change given, the first purchase by a woman, the first checked bag, shave, coffee (five cents), and even that

> the first man to fall asleep on one of the settees wore a light brown hat and a light overcoat. He said that he had been up all night waiting for the opening.

The people of Albany are *all* exceedingly proud of their elegant new Union Station.

Nine months later, on September 6, 1901, you're on a crew laying curbing up Broadway when President William McKinley is wounded in Buffalo by anarchist Leon Czolgosz. Vice-President Theodore Roosevelt rushes to Buffalo from Lake Champlain. But the Pres-ident rallies strongly, and by September 11, Roosevelt announces to the world that "the President's recovery is assured" and he leaves for the family camp on Mount Marcy in the Adirondacks. You wish *you* could go to a camp in the Adirondacks. Then, on Friday the thirteenth, McKinley's condition reverses.

Saturday morning, in the predawn dark, the Vice-President is rushed to Albany by special train. Awaiting word on whether to prepare to take the oath of office in the capital or proceed to Buffalo, Roosevelt remains locked in a private car out on Track Seven behind Union Station, well guarded against newsmen and additional conspirators. From the Broadway sidewalk, you look out back of the station, craning eagerly, history in the making! The order comes: the new President speeds west, without having set foot inside the new depot.

Will you see McKinley's body lying in state at the Capitol on its way back to Washington? No. The funeral train travels through Pennsylvania, bypassing Albany's black-draped, gleaming, nine-month-old Union Station.

Move forward in time again. In June 1923, Babe Ruth receives a hero's welcome at Union Station. In that same year you read about two new companies called Messerschmitt and Aeroflot. You're not sure you exactly understand their importance. But you *are* impressed when you read a few months later that Henry Ford has just produced his ten millionth car. You beam with satisfaction, having just chosen for your first automobile a Model T. You like having the freedom of an auto. True, you won't be using the trains much anymore, but . . . .

But . . . .

Well, the New York Central doesn't depend on just *your* business, right?

Alfred E. Perlman didn't agree. His railroad depended, for its survival, on regaining the patronage of all those individuals who were unconsciously turning to the car and the plane. Failing people's conversions back to the iron-wheeled faith, the Central had to preach to the converted of its own need to cut costs ruthlessly. "Oversize" downtown stations were an obvious target. "We're in a struggle for survival here and we intend to survive," said the company's general counsel, Gerald Dwyer, at a Public Service Commission hearing in Albany in August 1960. The Central claimed it could save half a million dollars a year by abandoning Union Station for a smaller, cross-river facility.

The PSC review went on and on. Almost a year later, the Commissioner said no:

> Upon the record, there is nothing to refute the conclusion that the bulk, if not all, of the savings predicted by the Central would be based not upon the discontinuance of the Albany station and the proposed relocation in Rensselaer but upon the fact that large savings can be accomplished through a modernization.

As Mayor Corning carried on his valiant efforts to save the downtown station, bad news came from the governor's mansion up on Eagle Street. Nelson A. Rockefeller decided in May 1962 that, as part of the immense South Mall state offices project (alternatively called Governor Nelson A. Rockefeller Empire State Plaza and "Rockefeller's Folly"), an arterial highway would run down the Hudson riverfront — over land occupied by the railroad tracks feeding Union Station.

The locomotive in this 1904
photo is an American Standard,
as was the Central's famous
No. 999, which in May 1893 first
conveyed human beings at over
one hundred miles per hour.

Because the arterial was part of an interstate highway construction project, the federal government would assume 90 percent and the State 10 percent of the cost of property taken from the railroad as well as the cost of the new passenger facilities erected elsewhere. Little wonder, then, that the New York Central allied itself with the highway-building interests on this particular issue. From this point on, although the battle seesawed and the PSC or the Mayor won an occasional reprieve, the outcome was no longer in doubt.

*December 14, 1966:* "UNION STATION SOLD TO STATE," the *Knickerbocker News* headlines ran. "Albany Depot Closing in 15 Months."

*October 12, 1967:* The PSC's demand of "a passenger stop facility" somewhere in downtown Albany led to yet another clash. Angry Central executives and attorneys in effect made their last counteroffer: a new station in Rensselaer. There was little choice for the PSC but to yield.

*December 2 and 3, 1967:* The Twentieth Century Limited made its last run through Albany.

*December 26, 1968:* With sublime understatement, a *Knickerbocker News* reporter wrote that

> When the ornate station on Broadway was opened, . . . it was a fashionable addition to the business district. At that time train travel was a growing business. . . . But with the coming of other forms of transportation, the station has grown much quieter. The Rensselaer station is of much less ornate design, with vertical and horizontal straight lines and large glass panels.

Another journalist more accurately called the Butler-type Rensselaer building "a gas station of a train station."

*Sunday, December 29, 1968:* The end of the line for Albany Union Station. Heavy snow grounded airplanes at the Albany airport and delayed buses; for the first time in years, Union Station was packed. Old-timers smiled wryly. When train No. 61, the unassuming successor to the legendary Twentieth Century, departed unceremoniously for Chicago, an era ended.

*December 30, 1968:* In an editorial, the *Knickerbocker News* spoke wistfully, but strongly and even prophetically:

> THOSE FOUR GOOD WALLS OF UNION STATION are monumental. The likes of them are seldom built nowadays. The proportions are noble. There is a dignity about the building even with its dilapidated interior and in its decayed setting. There is something there worth saving. . . . It should be restored together with its environs to become first an oasis and soon thereafter the center of a general area of renewal.

*1969, 1970, 1971:* Vandals sacked the building. With copper selling at 50 cents a pound, the roof flashings were quickly stripped. Water began seeping in. OGS, the Office of General Services, the State's custodian of surplus property, took possession.

*November 1971:* An auction was held on November 8, with the asking price for Union Station and its valuable downtown land a mere $320,000. No one bid. Another auction was held two weeks later. Not a single bidder came.

*1972, 1973, 1974, 1975, 1976, 1977, 1978:* The years passed. Countless salvation schemes surfaced and sank. Small trees sprouted on the roof. Moisture

In 1959, not even morning sunlight can dispel a dark future for Union Station. The New York Central is intent on closing its "obsolete" downtown depots.

Even diesel efficiency was power-
less to revive the failing rail industry. (The structure at left in
this 1959 photo is the steam
boiler plant.)

The time is late December 1968;
Union Station will close in just
a few days.

trickled in, gradually opening larger leaks in the roof and ceiling. Water began to stream in unimpeded, and soggy plaster gave way. Even structural steel eroded.

*1979:* The State erected a temporary roof to save the rapidly vanishing interior fabric. The wait for a buyer, or simply a dignified use, resumed.

*1980, 1981, 1982, 1983 . . . .*

*January 16, 1984:* IBM, which had been "seriously negotiating" with the City on renovation of Union Station as regional corporate offices, dropped its proposal.

A tired Albany banker listened to the IBM announcement on the evening news before going to bed. While shaving the next morning, he had an idea.

# The Team and the Plan

## NEW OWNER, NEW USE

In April 1959, when the *Trains* article on Union Station appeared, Peter D. Kiernan was managing the Rose & Kiernan insurance agency. Nineteen fifty-nine was an eventful year for Peter and Mary Agnes Kiernan, with the birth of their fifth child, Michael.

Peter, born in 1923, shared his own father's love of boating (the elder Kiernan rowed avidly until he was eighty), having taken it up as a teenager on the Hudson, where the national rowing championships had been held annually throughout much of the nineteenth century. He kept at rowing through his years "at the helm of the family business," as he puts it. Theirs was to become the largest privately owned insurance firm in the state. Kiernan's considerable energy, delight at working with people, renowned sense of humor, and pride of place made him a natural community leader; he soon sat on several boards of directors around Albany. He was doing well for himself, his large family, and the widely respected family business.

But he was not a banker. Thus it surprised him as well as others that as a very young member of the board at the State Bank of Albany he caught the eye of chairman Hollis E. Harrington. It may have been Kiernan's energy, or diligence in committee work, or an impressive presentation he delivered once while board chairman at Siena College. On this point as on other questions about his accomplishments, Kiernan characteristically sidesteps the issue. He eschews personal attention in general. Were it not for his large frame, he'd be a consummate coxswain.

Suddenly Kiernan *was* a banker. A holding company, the United Bank Corporation of New York, was created in January 1972, with the State Bank a founding partner and Kiernan a director.[3] He was quickly groomed by Harrington for succession, becoming president and CEO in 1974. For the next decade he showed that he'd learned his lessons well; this company, too, prospered. UBNY changed its name to Norstar Bancorp on January 4, 1982, and continued growing prodigiously. Good years lay ahead. Kiernan had indeed climbed into a winning shell.

But, quite gradually, an unexpected problem arose for Norstar. At the modern but unprepossessing offices on Western Avenue, the third floor was approaching capacity under the weight of the data processing department's expanding hardware installation and reams of paper. Although there was not yet any danger of collapse, the company would have to figure out what to do about finding more space — soon.

On Monday, January 16, 1984, Kiernan was watching the evening news on television. "In the latest of a long series of disappointments for the City," the commentator reported, "the IBM Corporation has announced it is no longer considering buying and renovating Albany's Union Station as regional corporate offices."

An Albany native, Kiernan had had many occasions to stride through Union Station. When he, like so many others, left for the service by train, the place

In 1977, there were trees growing
on the roof.  By 1984, the de-
terioration had been stabilized,
but the job ahead was still
monumental.

hummed. Now, in the winter of 1983-84, the station was shabby, its neighborhood dubious, and the word for downtown Albany was "depressed." In the city center, building projects were suspended for lack of tenants, or financing, or both. Development plans seemed no more than pipe dreams.

These thoughts were surely on Kiernan's mind as he drifted into sleep that Monday night. He was a community-oriented Albanian, the chairman of the larger of the two Fortune 500 companies headquartered in the city. Albany was trying to shake off the onus of decline, trying to identify prospects for a meaningful future. It was taking years for people even to accept the permanency of the amazing Empire State Plaza, former Governor Nelson Rockefeller's thwarted attempt at immortality, looming like a broken oath above a city plagued by ugly blight and urban woes. Everyone in city planning and urban development knew that after sixteen years of abandonment Union Station was the potential catalyst. But they also knew that, in a city where 71 percent of the property was tax exempt, salvation lay in the private sector.

As Kiernan shaved Tuesday morning, January 17, 1984, he decided to go see the Mayor. They had a casual chat in which enthusiasm kept roiling the calm surface. "I could feel a certain shortness of breath," Thomas M. Whalen III recalls. "Finally, I just said out loud, to Peter and myself, 'Merry Christmas, Tommy.'" Erastus Corning II had died the previous May, after choosing Whalen to be his successor and leaving him the most debt-ridden city in the state.

Whalen also inherited a broad agenda of unfinished business, not the least of which was Union Station. He'd shared Corning's commitment to keeping Union Station open, ever since he'd gotten out of the service in March 1959 and gone to work for Albany's most venerable law firm. His office was a few blocks from the train station which he, like almost everyone in Albany, had used and taken for granted many, many times.

Their chat was brief. When Kiernan left, he drove down to look at the boarded-up, run-down station. Sitting in front of the magnificent but forlorn building, he recalled an idea he'd discussed with a contractor friend shortly after the station closed in 1968: why not make an insurance center out of the place? Cars could drive in through the Broadway arches and park inside the waiting-room space, and a floor could be inserted over the parking area. . . . The contractor, James P. "Pat" McKenna, had even approached Mayor Corning with the idea, but the City had wanted too much for the building then. Kiernan smiled, winked at the building, and drove back to work.

---

The April 11, 1984, announcement caused a sensation. Joining Kiernan under the frame of the station's front canopy were Whalen and Governor Mario M. Cuomo. The three orated with gusto. Cuomo's "the hub of the Albany-that-was, the heart of the Albany-to-be"; Whalen's "Erastus, we did it!" (with Erastus Corning III looking on); and Kiernan's "What started out as good citizenship now promises to make good business sense as well" added to the universal jubilation which filled Downtown.

"UNION STATION REBORN," the *Times-Union* shouted on April 12. "Norstar reveals renovation plans," the paper assured the doubters who had seen proposal after proposal vaporize since 1968. This time, something would happen.

What splendid irony! Norstar Bancorp's predecessor was the State Bank of Albany, the very same bank which had financed the Erie Canal and the Mohawk & Hudson! The bank whose former loan officer in charge of railroad investments, Erastus Corning, had founded the New York Central, the railroad which built Union Station. The railroad which, back in the dark days of the late 1950s, had threatened another Corning and practically everyone else with abandonment of Union Station. How ironic, that that railroad had been spliced ignominiously into the Penn Central in January 1968, had seen the station it detested closed "forever" in December of the same year, and then had itself vanished within three years . . . while the once-great railroad's granite mausoleum hunkered down to await redemption.

This time, it would happen. Peter Kiernan's energy, affection for the old place, and nascent commitment to an extraordinary community project would breed necessary enthusiasm among important backers, the Governor and the Mayor being two of the earliest to sign on. Union Station would open its doors again as Norstar Plaza, a powerful catalyst for the revitalization of a neighborhood, a downtown, and a city's pride.

## ARCHITECTS, BUILDERS, AND ENGINEERS

To the cynics, Union Station was a nearly irreparable sinkhole into which well-oiled Norstar would pour its prodigious assets. Even the optimistic began to wonder. While press releases extolled the company's

eagerness to get on with the renovation, the management team began soberly to assess the magnitude of the job. What if they dug into the structure and found it hopelessly deteriorated? Would the place end up a well-publicized bad investment?

At the offices of Norstar's architect of choice, Einhorn Yaffee Prescott PC,[4] a couple of blocks down Broadway from Union Station, uncertainty did not trouble Steven L. Einhorn. The 42-year-old cofounder of EYP was confident the building could be saved, and saved handsomely. Einhorn knew Union Station inside out.

Our April 1959 milepost in the Union Station story found Einhorn a junior in high school. ("April?" he replies to the question of what he was doing then. "I was playing baseball.") He was dreaming, he recalls, of becoming a surgeon — "a great surgeon." Instead, in college his interest in science and people resulted in a dual major, architecture and sociology. He and Eric Yaffee opened an office in 1972 and started doing small-interior work. They also took a cooking course. At a charity auction, their donation (a catered black-tie dinner for six) drew the top bid of the night, from Mr. and Mrs. Donald McD. Slingerland of the State Bank of Albany. When the big night arrived, Einhorn played chauffeur and maître d' for the Slingerlands and their guests — two of whom were the Kiernans.

Five years after that improbable introduction, Einhorn's name came up again at United Bank of New York when the firm successfully bid for the design of the holding company's corporate office space in the new headquarters building at 1450 Western Avenue. Einhorn Yaffee Prescott had, in the meantime, also done an analysis of possible reuses for the then-derelict

The April 11, 1984, press conference: Mayor Thomas Whalen speaking, Governor Mario Cuomo, and Peter Kiernan. Standing in the rear, to the right of Cuomo, is Erastus Corning III.

Union Station for the State. They subsequently completed an analysis of the building, *Union Station: A Historic Structure Report,* also commissioned by the State. This definitive study bonded EYP's name to the station (the temporary roof and other repairs performed by OGS in 1979 closely followed recommendations found in the *Historic Structure Report*).

In the earliest discussions of the Plaza with the architect, Norstar accepted an option which escalated complications and risk in the project: the "fast-track" method of planning. Instead of waiting for the submission, revision, approval, and completion of a full set of working drawings and blueprints, the owner wanted to push for the earliest possible completion date. Fast-tracking would allow a set of plans to be finished quickly in order for work to get briskly under way. But those plans would then be continuously revised according to what turned up, what went wrong, and what someone at any stage might decide to change.

Thus Einhorn's familiarity with the building only partially offset the fact that the architects, like the contractors submitting bids, would often have to make estimates simply by taking an educated guess. Planning and construction were to proceed simultaneously!

Einhorn favored the fast-track method, which had served him well in projects like hospital renovations and additions, where the facility must remain in operation during construction. He realized there could be plenty of surprises in this complex renovation, but he concurred with the owner in setting an early completion date and shooting for it. Like Kiernan, Einhorn saw a worthwhile goal and accepted the challenge.

Fast-track planning offered several benefits to offset the risk and complication:

> It would allow Norstar to reduce the interest charges on the financing of the project
>
> It would allow a completion date of summer 1986, coinciding appropriately with Albany's festive Tricentennial celebration
>
> It would impose an absolute deadline for moving in, which was seen as a positive factor in holding the mammoth job to a schedule, as the massive new computer system had to be ordered with considerable lead time and the data processing facility would have to be ready.

Fast-track planning creates the momentum to overcome inevitable obstacles and impediments. A palpable sense of "RUSH!" about the job would be a hefty implement in everyone's toolbox. Peter Kiernan, the legend went, got what he wanted by getting the best out of his people. For over thirty years he'd learned to wield the magic power of The Imminent Deadline. "If you want a job done well," goes the paradoxical adage, "give it to a busy person." Kiernan and Einhorn would create busy people.

In a way, much of the preliminary analysis of existing conditions was already done. EYP's *Union Station: A Historic Structure Report,* prepared in 1979 by Project Architect Paul Scoville, filled nearly two hundred pages with thorough research on the work of the builders of 1900 along with a meticulous examination of the building's present (1979) physical condition. The report laid a comprehensive foundation for the program of modification ahead.

Steven Einhorn.

Peter Kiernan.

From left, Steven Einhorn, John
Myers, and Tom Birdsey.

At Einhorn Yaffee Prescott, Tom Birdsey was named Project Manager; John Myers became the Job Captain. Einhorn himself kept close to all design developments as they unfolded and supervised the inevitable broad-stroke changes to design and process. "An architect's problems," says Einhorn, "are inversely proportional to the amount of preparation of the documents; the more we have to work with, the fewer surprises we'll run into. But with the fast-track approach, we wouldn't be starting with extensive documentation. This would be almost an experimental project."

Birdsey agrees: "When you fast-track the reconstruction of an existing building in bad shape, you learn what's there as you go along. So every subcontracting package departs from a point which can't be predicted much in advance. Just think about it." And Myers points out that the questions depend on the answers, not vice versa: "If the designs are not finalized, all you can do is guess at what preparations have to be accomplished in a particular area. This was really fifty renovations, not just one. We had to mold the design decisions around what we thought would exist at each subsequent stage."

Where were Birdsey and Myers back in the spring of 1959? In school. Probably sketching street and track plans and passenger depots as practice for future submissions to America's railroads. Messrs. John McManus, Fred Longe, and Donald Brockwehl, on the other hand, were hard at work. These three, who had seen the Depression as kids, in 1947 formed the construction firm whose name came from their last initials, MLB, Inc. Peter Kiernan, Sr., had provided the insurance bonding for the company's first job. Thus began a cordial and longstanding relationship.

Over the years, MLB built and remodeled a number of branch bank buildings for State Bank and then for Norstar.

In August 1984, the owners and architects dropped by MLB's offices in the suburb of Latham, in an industrial park near the airport, to talk about Norstar Plaza. As construction managers for a job this size, MLB would assemble a considerable team of supervisors, engineers, carpenters, and laborers — in addition to several dozen subcontractors and all their personnel. McManus and Project Coordinator (later Project Manager) Ed Grey would oversee the construction project directly; eventually Vice-President of Operations James Dawsey would assume responsibility for control and scheduling. Grey, in turn, would have a project engineer (Don Luce, followed by Kim Straight, and later Norman Gervais) and a superintendent, Sam Boschelli, through whom he'd coordinate with the foremen of the carpenters and laborers. There would be a project scheduler to handle the computer printouts, an engineer dealing with change requests, and one person dedicated to coordination between mechanical and electrical subcontracting activities. Three field office personnel would join these people in the two trailers set up alongside the building. Thus several supervisors and as many as forty carpenters and laborers would be on the job — and that was just the construction management contingent.

Ed Grey would be the ombudsman, always around, always knowledgeable as to the latest status of the project. Grey had been with MLB since 1963, managing since 1972. Although he'd been on some big jobs (including the Niagara Power Project, back in 1959), this one was sure to be a particular challenge. Did he know what he was in for? "I knew it was going to be tough, at any given stage," he says, "to stay out ahead of the next construction sequences that were getting under way."

Fast-track planning required a huge design staff to keep up. If management let scheduling slip, the entire project would begin to founder. As project manager, Grey would have limited time to review the architects' bid packages before they went out; there would not be time to revise and nail down all the details. Hundreds, possibly thousands of change requests would be coming in, each nudging up price, pushing back scheduling, setting back work in related and dependent areas. The mind-boggling thing was that there were almost no criteria to help gauge how many changes lay ahead. They'd just have to dig in and see what they uncovered as they went.

## ARTISANS

Let's move somewhat ahead of the chronology to introduce two key figures here. Saving Union Station meant restoring turn-of-the-century cast iron and vast reaches of ornamental and figurine plaster, the likes of which were not available at any neighborhood do-it-yourself store in 1984. On the initial "shopping list" which Norstar presented to the architects, the number two item (after the top priority of doubling floor space) was to restore the deeply coffered, elaborately sculpted ceiling. To be eligible for historic-preservation tax credits and for federal funding assistance, the project was sure to require restoration of that striking feature of the station interior. But fully one-third of the ceiling plaster was rotten or completely missing, and perhaps 90 percent of the entire ceiling seemed to require repair of supporting structures and plaster restoration. Was it worth saving, or should the ceiling be demolished and the original patterns be replicated? If the ceiling were to be reproduced, how? With what materials? More to the point, with what processes? Who was around in 1984 who had that knowledge?

Job Captain John Myers donned his EYP hard hat, loaded his 35mm camera, grabbed a flashlight and clipboard, and climbed up into the station attic on August 8, 1984. His earlier employment had taught him a little about ornamental plaster, so he went looking. It was terrifically hot up there, in most places dark, except where subdued light from the vacant lobby and offices reflected upward into the attic through holes opened by years of erosion. Crawling across structures of dubious strength, with an occasional peep through ragged-edged holes down 50-some feet to the waiting room floor (onto which plaster debris would fall periodically), edging up and down over the backsides of mounds of ancient plaster, in a stuffy, mildewed space, Myers cast his flashlight beam over the keying of the plaster which remained. Was any of it still being held solidly in place, or was the entire ceiling beyond salvaging?

He thought it looked pretty good, except for the lowest flat portions where water had had the chance to "pond" for sixteen years. But he needed an expert opinion. Back in his office, he cracked open Sweet's fifteen-volume vendors catalog and made a few calls.

There are not many people around who practice handcraft in the age of mass production and what's-the-bottom-line construction. Of the few businesses in America which still produce ornamental plaster, fewer still shun foams and such to work instead with the costlier, high-quality materials that Norstar would demand. And of that small number of manufacturers, Myers discovered from his phone calls, only one was willing to come to Albany and climb up in the attic of a decrepit train station for an inspection.

Bob Sweeney fits the notion of an inveterate marcher-to-a-different-drummer. Pretty much on his own since age fifteen, with no chance of affording college, he went directly from high school into the first of a string of intriguing occupations (running a laundromat). "Most of them involved using my hands," Sweeney says. He seemed always to be in some one-man business or another; he's pleased to estimate that he has drawn perhaps six months of paychecks in his entire life, "and only one unemployment check. That so bothered me, I never went back to get the others I was entitled to."

Sweeney savors a challenge: "I like doing things which I don't believe I can do." One day he got cajoled into trying to repair a pineapple ornament atop his daughter's mahogany bed. "It gave me horrendous satisfaction," he recalls with a characteristically sly grin. He looked for more such chances to "play" with wood. That led to furniture restoration and thence the creation of Dovetail, Inc., specialists in ornamental repair and, ultimately, plaster restoration. The company grew and soon occupied what was informally known in Lowell, Mass. as "The Sweeney Building," one of the many nineteenth-century mills being rehabilitated during the late seventies in that canaled city.

Sweeney was willing to come to Albany because he maintained an attitude ("it probably *can* be saved") which "gives great relief to the client." This attitude and the ability to follow through on it have earned Dovetail a topflight reputation in the restoration field. (He was also curious, he now confesses even more slyly, to see if it could be saved.) Was Myers right? Could the ceiling be rebuilt around much of what was in place? If not, what were the alternatives? As for the plaster medallions and busts, well, they might be another matter. So too was the question of installing the castings which would eventually be produced. Myers had to find another artisan. On Sweeney's referral, he did — Ben Soep.

Ben Soep wanted to be an artist, and studied accordingly. But on his discharge at the end of the Second World War, he, like Sweeney, had to find a way to scratch out a living. Soep took over a defunct company and made cabinets for the new 7-inch television sets of the day. Then, during an aluminum shortage, he found a clever way to use surplus wood dowels to make ersatz TV antennas. He dabbled with rubberized aluminum, neoprene, copper naphthanol . . . .

His painting business was still small in 1959; the following year would change that as he'd do the full interior restoration of the Colonial Theater in Boston and make a name for himself ("Ben Soep: Commercial Painting Plus," he smiles). Some impressive restorations and decorating projects followed, including Faneuil Hall and, currently, the new Rowe's Wharf complex.

We'll meet Bob Sweeney and Ben Soep again in the following pages. But there's one last group of players to introduce in the Norstar Plaza drama.

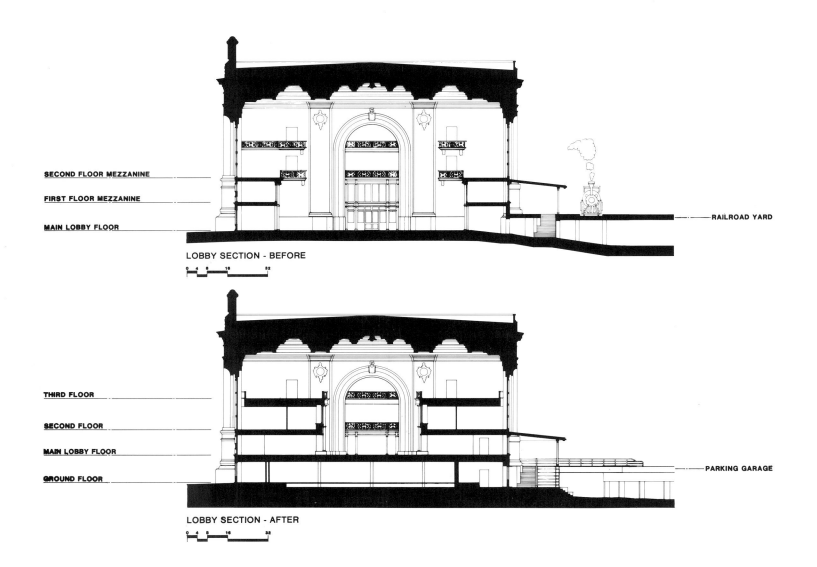

SECOND FLOOR MEZZANINE

FIRST FLOOR MEZZANINE

MAIN LOBBY FLOOR

RAILROAD YARD

LOBBY SECTION - BEFORE

0  4  8    16        32

THIRD FLOOR

SECOND FLOOR

MAIN LOBBY FLOOR

GROUND FLOOR

PARKING GARAGE

LOBBY SECTION - AFTER

0  4  8    16        32

These views of the south end of
the station show the ingenious
solution to doubling usable floor
space without destroying a sense
of grandeur in the lobby.  Note
also the sensitively set height of
the parking garage.

## OVERSEERS AND REVIEWERS

The new owner, the architect, the construction engineer, the craftsman — these are the professionals who get the glory in a major building project. But many other professionals do their (perhaps less glamorous but no less essential) jobs well, too.

The Albany Union Station story is one in which, amazingly, everybody won. This is because everyone cared. To illustrate the conscientiousness which even the unheralded participants brought to the project, let's consider two aspects of the task which might easily be overlooked: the magic and the money.

Fresh from the pressing search for more room for their data processing department, Norstar's management was mindful of allowing for as much future expansion as was practical. From the very first inspection of Union Station, they saw clearly that the available floor space was nowhere near sufficient for *present* needs, much less for those of a company growing some 30 percent yearly. No one could stand in that 56-foot-high waiting room and fail to think that the volume could be put to better use.

Almost any approach to getting more usable floor space out of that void would diminish the overall impression of size and grandeur felt by every traveler and visitor in Union Station. No matter that other railroad stations had larger waiting rooms; the point was that the definable character of *this* place (as would be true of any sizable station building) stemmed in great part from its spaciousness and the way in which spaciousness contributed to that particular building's aura of elegance.

Union Station had not been designed for office use. It was designed, in the phrase of Pulitzer Prize-winning Albany author William Kennedy, as "a gift

of munificence" from railroad to city and citizenry. For the countless people who moved in and out of the building over the years, beyond the handsome façade Union Station was essentially a huge and ornate waiting room (*their* huge and ornate waiting room). That impression of grand space *was* a principal, and very personal, attraction of Union Station. It would have to be retained. How, then, would the architect and owner increase existing floor space (avoiding annexation of any sort) without irretrievably diminishing the magic imparted by that fine interior space?

Einhorn found an answer. He proposed to insert a new floor throughout the entire building, thus raising the effective lobby level one complete story. The remaining ground-level space could be designed as a single unit, easily amenable to the security and access control which a big and vital data processing center would require. Inserting a new floor from north wall to south wall would also create four stories in the three-story wings (the original ground-floor quarters in the wings — baggage room to the north, restaurant to the south — were twice the height of the floors above). And if the cast-iron gallery façades were moved upward and inward, the mezzanines would gain space. The result would be nearly twice the existing floor area, in a building whose exterior would not be visibly changed. From an engineering standpoint, the plan was challenging but feasible. Now the developers had to determine if the same would be true from a preservation standpoint.

At the complex of offices in the Empire State Plaza, on the twentieth floor of Agency Building 1, is the office of Julia S. (Julie) Stokes, Deputy Commissioner for Historic Preservation, part of the State's Office of

Parks, Recreation and Historic Preservation (commonly called SHPO, pronounced to rhyme with "hippo"). Although Stokes reported to Commissioner Orin Lehman, she was in effect the person who made day-to-day decisions on the Norstar Plaza project.

SHPO is a fulcrum in a contest of wills. It receives, from the Interior Department's Philadelphia office, explicit guidelines from the United States Secretary of the Interior on how historic-preservation projects are to be conducted. Developers, companies, and municipalities throughout New York State bring proposals for historic-preservation, adaptive-use renovations of every sort of building, for every sort of purpose. If projects are to qualify for investment tax credits, the Interior Department expects compliance with its complex guidelines. Petitioners, for their part, expect a free hand to achieve the objectives of their particular reuse projects. In crude terms, Washington has the power to write the regulations; Philadelphia has the clout to stop the tax credits; but the developers have the bucks to save the buildings. In that perceived alignment, there is much room for dispute. Thus New York State's SHPO acts at different times as liaison, advocate, enforcer, and supplicant.

New York State is an acknowledged leader in supporting and funding historic-preservation projects, and so Stokes's office has set a number of precedents in historic-tax-credit cases. Philadelphia is less able to bend the rules to encourage pioneering (read: unprecedented) efforts in historic preservation. Thus Julie Stokes often finds herself caught in the crossfire — sometimes actually taking sides with the owners and architects in order to expand the terms of the permissible in the next round. In selfish terms, it's important for her to establish a successful track record for her own office.

Thus popular notions may sometimes be highly simplistic. The National Register of Historic Places, for example, is not sacrosanct, not a perfect shelter as people sometimes imagine; Union Station was on the Register in 1971, but the proposed terms of sale at the two OGS auctions did *not* preclude demolition of the building. Similarly, the "bureaucrats" are not always the bad guys, thwarting the noble aspirations of the "preservationists." The owner and architect may call the staff at SHPO "the preservation people" (as in, "I wonder if the preservation people will buy this"), but they realize that the relationship is complex and definitely worth cultivating.

Julie Stokes was not always a deputy commissioner, or even a bureaucrat. An Albany-area high school student in Union Station's watershed year of 1959, married in a Detroit suburb, she was a housewife when her husband transferred to Saratoga Springs, just north of Albany, in 1966. She was a trailblazer. An activist, Stokes was soon campaigning to save Saratoga's historic Canfield Casino. She was directly involved in the formation of the Saratoga Springs Preservation Foundation and was hired as its first executive director. "I wanted to be on site, right down there at the doorstep," she reminisces, "making sure that what was supposed to be happening was happening. I was a street preservationist."

In 1984 she received the deputy commissioner appointment. Union Station was then just one of a number of important buildings awaiting their fates. The SHPO staff had already heard a litany of plans for the station — from aquarium to bowling hall of fame. But after Peter Kiernan came forward with his proposal, the perception of the train station's value changed abruptly. Commitment was solidifying.

The SHPO staff knew the building from earlier reports and surveys. They saw the big picture, the importance of this project to the capital city of New York State. They saw, too, the Deputy Commissioner's enthusiasm for a project which already had the highly visible endorsement of the Mayor and the Governor. The staff, too, assumed a commitment to the success of this historic renovation.

That was the magic. Then there was the money. Norstar Bancorp may have been a banking company, but it was unrealistic to expect the firm to shell out cash for the entire job. One of the first items to appear on the "shopping list" given to Einhorn Yaffee Prescott by Norstar was tax credits. The building was on the National Register of Historic Places. If the project met federal guidelines for proper historic preservation, then the owner would be entitled to deduct fully 25 percent of the renovation costs from federal taxes due, dollar-for-dollar. Federal tax credits were bundled, however, with regulatory consequences, such that opting for the tax credits meant scrutiny and exacting compliance from a number of agencies.[5] The decision was not to be taken lightly. Nevertheless, Kiernan saw the investment tax credits as an important part of the presentation he made to the board of directors on March 21, 1984, to solicit their approval for the project.

The State and the City also got involved in the financing at this earliest stage. Mayor Whalen's excitement at the Norstar offer must be viewed in the context of Albany's ongoing struggle to overcome a despairing downtown situation. "One must view the City's eagerness to promote the project," says Norstar's General Counsel, Vice-President and Secretary Harry P. Meislahn, "in the perspective of the winter of 1983-1984. There was *nothing* going on."

The City stood to gain a great deal from the renovation. The catalytic effect of this major downtown rehabilitation was valuable beyond dollar calculation, but there were immediate and tangible benefits, too, such as the return of the property to the City's limited tax rolls. Although a number of development schemes had proposed public use of Union Station, the consensus in and around city government was that private development, or a public-private joint effort, made more sense. It was sure to induce more response from the business community than would yet another government-facility adaptation of an existing building (even assuming that such an adaptation could be a certifiable historic rehab).

There had been talk, for years, of using Union Station as a civic center. One quite ambitious and intriguing variant on the idea was to make of the station the grand entrance to a civic center which would literally straddle the waterfront arterial highway, thus connecting the Corning Preserve recreational land along the river to the sidewalks of downtown Albany.

A fundamental problem with all such schemes remained the funding. Here, at long last, the City had a reliable private developer with an attractive plan for public-private collaboration and a viable financing arrangement. That had never been the case in the past, and no one knew how long it might be before something comparably attainable might arise.

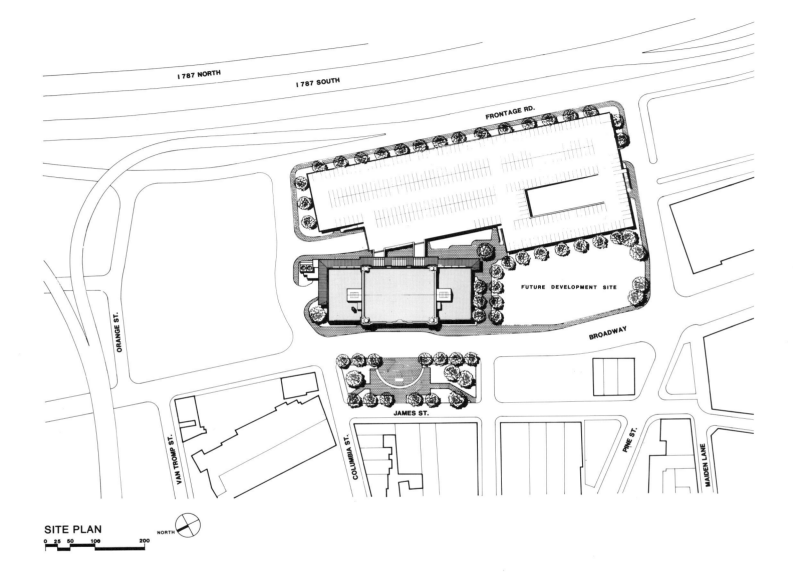

I 787 NORTH

I 787 SOUTH

FRONTAGE RD.

ORANGE ST.

FUTURE DEVELOPMENT SITE

BROADWAY

VAN TROMP ST.

COLUMBIA ST.

JAMES ST.

PINE ST.

MAIDEN LANE

**SITE PLAN**

0  25  50  100          200

NORTH

This architectural site plan
shows the parking garage, Tricentennial Park, and details of
Norstar Plaza and environs in
true proportion.

Cars and roads surround the station in 1979. In the background the Hudson River bridge carries Amtrak trains to and from the "Albany" station in Rensselaer.

The proposed Norstar Plaza financing package included a request for a UDAG (Urban Development Action Grant) and for issuance of bonds through IDA, the City's Industrial Development Agency, with Norstar providing the remainder through funding of its own choosing. The make-up of the package was not determined by formal stipulation, nor even by convention. This was to be an unprecedented public-private collaboration, and as such the interested parties could pick and choose from a number of sources of funding.

They were also obliged to hammer out a bargain which would leave everyone satisfied. Thus the Mayor and City representatives worked out an exchange by which Norstar would also cooperate in realizing some of the City's plans. Norstar agreed to build an 800-car parking garage and then sell it to the City for use by the Parking Authority. Employees would surely rent a considerable number of spaces on a monthly basis. Again, everyone was happy. Norstar would get a compatibly-designed parking facility, with the convenience of covered access to the building, and the City would benefit from committed use of costly parking development, financing through a bond offering, and less strain on cash flow.

The parties also discussed creation of a park facing Norstar Plaza, to be dedicated in 1986, the City's tricentennial year. The project would be a groundbreaker in more ways than one, as will be seen later. Through all these negotiations and planning sessions, one thing remained clear. The Norstar Plaza project

was exceptionally popular. Virtually everyone was behind it, practically no opposition had been broached,[6] and anyone even indirectly associated with it wanted it to succeed. This hardly fits the stereotype of obstruction from Office X or foot-dragging at Agency Y. The people in public offices and governmental agencies, just as much as everyone else, wanted Union Station to come back to life.

# The Groundwork

## SITE AND STREETS

"Environmental Impact Statement" is one of those terms the layperson occasionally hears but which lacks material reality. The Statement (hereafter, the EIS) is a real document, though, a part of all such major construction projects, generated for hands-on use. For the casual reader, it's sometimes surprisingly interesting.

The two-inch-thick EIS No. 840439 shows the direction of the winter and summer winds, sources of road noise, emissions from a nearby power plant, and the 100- and 500-year flood boundaries.[7] It counts pedestrian movements along various sidewalks and shows which way cars turn in a typical business day. It tells the reader about rusted cast iron, reusable wooden doors, iron stairways which hang in space and lead to nowhere, the condition of the original flooring, and the location of plaster faults.

The EIS details where the owner's money is coming from, and where it's expected to go. It shows that Union Station sits just outside one of the six gates of the Stockade of 1695, a little to the north of "a great gun to clear a galley."[8] And it tells what the soil is like if one were to go out in back of the station and bore a hole 50 feet down. It tells much, much more.

Because the owner is applying for federal funding and because the building is on the National Register of Historic Places, an EIS is obligatory. It gives the owner and architect comprehensive knowledge of (and, following two lengthy public comment periods, permission to begin preparing) the site of Norstar Plaza and its parking garage. The EIS is a fascinating document.

The environmental analysis is also the principal reason why the actual work did not get under way until more than a year after Peter Kiernan's memorable shave. The "scoping" meeting with MLB in August 1984 initiated the process which led to publication of the EIS by Hershberg and Hershberg, consulting engineers and land surveyors. But until final approval of the EIS came on February 11, 1985, all that MLB could do was remove falling plaster and let subcontractors remove the asbestos insulation on piping wherever it was visible. Otherwise, the site was quiet.

In addition to the station and its immediate property, the "site" included the large parcel of land behind (to the east and southeast) and the parcel of land just to the north of the building, both of which then served as parking lots. Even before IBM's Union Station negotiations of late 1983, the City had attempted to stimulate interest in the area by proposing to build a parking garage, a cube structure of eight stories, on the southeast corner of the land behind the station. Once Norstar's commitment was firm and the State and the City had swapped ownership of the two parcels, the cube garage yielded to a low and long design more reminiscent of passenger train platforms, more sensitive to the vista at the back of the building, and more an integral part of Norstar Plaza.

That 1983 cube garage had prompted a Cultural Resources Survey, which contributed to the EIS information on what was actually on the site below the surface. From documents and drillings, the Survey identified what strata existed on the site and whether the proposed development would irreparably disturb deposits of archaeological interest. The conclusion was that the New York Central had already done about as much damage to the area in its own grading and building as could possibly be done now through a few shallow pile-drivings for the garage. The light again turned green.

Bruce Hiser, landscape architect, was asked by Einhorn Yaffee Prescott[9] to design the grading and designate the greenery for the Norstar Plaza site. Hiser quickly determined that Columbia Street was too tight; it would have to be rerouted. In the station days, Columbia Street had actually dipped to pass under the railroad tracks emerging from the north end of the station platforms. When the tracks and bridging were torn up in 1969, Columbia Street rose to nearly the same level as Broadway, but it still was a bit odd and uneven. Backing trucks in and out of the Norstar Plaza loading dock area would be difficult. So Hiser proposed to "straighten and level" the gradual rise of Columbia Street, actually moving it over a few feet as well. Such are the unexpected demands of historic preservation!

The idea seemed straightforward enough, but it generated considerable ramifications, from traffic studies at the Office of City Planning to consideration of potential difficulties in fire-truck access. While lawyers and engineers grappled with those concerns, Hiser turned his attention to the trees.

EYP's original sketches were a good starting point, but Hiser wanted to thin out the plantings along the highway side (he ultimately decided that there would be no trees atop the parking garage). The garage itself was going to be a rather simple structure, "nicely textured, but from a design viewpoint it was a restrained façade," Hiser says. He proposed to break up that street-level stretch with what would functionally be snow-unloading docks and a number of pine trees. Low along the façade, he suggested hardy, easily maintained juniper bushes to add grace to the garage.

Even the curbs came under Hiser's attention. There were still remnants of the 1900-era granite curbing which shared the tint of Union Station's pink Milford granite. Unfortunately, there was not enough to be reused satisfactorily, and it would have exceeded the budget to bring in more, so Hiser had to ask the builders to resort to plain old granite instead.

Meanwhile, out in back, the parking garage began to take shape. On this project there were subcontractors with colorful histories. Peter Callanan, the grandson of an Irish immigrant, started the Callanan Road Improvement Company in 1883. He was so devoted to his craft that he wrote a booklet in 1889, "Roads and Road Making," in which he declared that "Americans ride much more than Europeans," but that the "vastly inferior" condition of our roads was "not mere shortsightedness, it is almost criminal negligence." He then went on to explain how to build a good road.

In 1948, a dentist, the son of the company's dynamite expert, dropped out six months after starting practice and came to work for Callanan Industries. Alfonso Marcelle, "Doc" to his construction buddies, eventually became chairman of the company and then its owner in 1983. A diverse and successful company,

Callanan Industries now dug in to build Norstar a garage. Doc Marcelle threw himself into the job with his usual gusto. Like other members of the project, he got rather romantically involved with the building, often taking a sidetrip inside to see what was happening. He and Peter Kiernan had been close friends for a number of years, and Doc clearly shared the vision of what the place was going to become.

## CLEANOUT AND TEARDOWN

It wasn't at all easy to see what the place would become when one saw what it still *was* in the winter of 1984-1985.

The first workers to enter Union Station and begin the job were from Tom and Antoinette ("Toni") Cristo's demolition company.[10] In October 1984 they began removing what remained of the terrazzo flooring to expose the pipes beneath so that a qualified firm, Asbestos Containment, could begin removing pipe covering (as well as cement-asbestos boards at other locations).[11] The toxin had been used much more extensively in Union Station than was estimated. By law, though, the demolition people were prohibited from doing any actual asbestos removal whatsoever. In complying with guidelines from the Environmental Protection Agency and other regulators, Asbestos Containment would be entitled (for want of a better word) to come in, seal off the work area, establish protective measures, detach the aging pipe lagging, bag and can it, ship it out, clean up, and recertify the area.

Once that was done, Toni Cristo's bulldozer returned to rip up the flooring, while the jackhammers and torches attacked all the old concrete infill flooring and unneeded steel trusses elsewhere in the building. The contract said, in so many words, to "gut the interior to the envelope of the building" — the exterior walls.

Even this first step of the process — go in, tear out, clean up — reflected the pervasive complication of fast-track planning. The bulldozer was ready; but how much had to be taken out? The worn-out terrazzo floor, of course, had to go. There were pipes running who-knew-where under the floor. How far down would the demolition have to go? How much of the old foundation was redeemable? Where would the new foundations be? Where would the framing for the new floor insertion be required?

The answers came from a surprising confluence of design factors. First, the historic-preservation concerns about retaining grandeur and proportion in the lobby determined at what height the new lobby level (and thus the ceiling of the data processing area) would be inserted. Next, the 100-year flood plane decreed how low the computer system could safely rest. Finally, IBM recommended that the false flooring for the new mainframe be erected at least 24 inches above the actual ground level so as to accommodate the massive cable runs and new equipment. Norstar and EYP had been considering the same 12-inch height as at 1450 Western Avenue — the extra foot or so on which IBM insisted would leave the facility uncomfortably cramped. Everyone compromised on 18 inches, and the bulldozer began scraping off a few inches of rubble from the original foundation.

Also, plans called for two tunnels running the length of the lobby area, penetrating just past the archways at both ends, through which the heating and electrical systems for the building would pass. These two cuts, each eight feet tall for service access, also needed to be bulldozed. While digging the tunnels, Cristo and the masonry subcontractor, Clifford H. Quay & Sons, were amazed to strike granite five feet beneath the main floor at street level — apparently the paving from Montgomery Street, which had disappeared in the construction of Union Station in 1898!

## PLASTER, PART 1

After his exploration of the attic and ceiling, John Myers phoned a number of people before he found Dovetail. He described his findings and sent photos to Sweeney, who wrote back on August 16: "It appears that the ceiling is in salvageable condition, with the major damage . . . in the beam bottoms" (those wide flats where water sat for years) and the radial ornament and detail around the six tall windows.

The first thing to do was arrange a site inspection, from which Sweeney could prepare a report for EYP and Norstar. He and an assistant came to Albany from Lowell, Mass., on September 11. Myers vividly recalls Sweeney's first words as they stepped into the waiting room and looked up. "Well," Sweeney said slowly and softly, his voice echoing nevertheless in the empty waiting room, "it's a lot worse than I thought it was."

They made their way up to the attic to see the backside. From this privileged vantage point, one which, unfortunately, the millions of users of Union Station never enjoyed, the true scale of this once splendid ceiling is very clear. Most waiting room visitors would look up, see a ceiling way up high with lots of details, say "Wow," and head for the train. From up above, one realizes that the box-within-a-box-within-a-box coffer design takes up tremendous space, vertically (the unappreciated aspect) as well as horizontally. Standing at the lowest edge of the coffers (the bottom beams, as seen from below), even a professional basketball player would have to jump up to get a glimpse over the topmost point of the coffer towards the other vast mounds. The three largest mounds are squares some 35 feet on a side; there are nine coffers in all. If the wow-saying traveler were able to see all this from above, he or she would certainly linger a while and then head, permanently impressed, for the train.

Moving through the dim, ravaged, but spiritually welcoming space above the coffers, Sweeney was in his realm. He needed only ten minutes to confirm Myers's appraisal. When original plastering is done, over a meshlike lath of wire attached to iron hangers, the "brown coat" (which is essentially cement) is applied in such a way that it squeezes past the lath and curls around to fill the space behind. The effect is called "keying" and is comparable to the dovetail joint in fine woodworking. (Sweeney points out that a good plasterer can effect solid keying to support an exterior face as thin as one-eighth inch.) Thus anchored uniformly over even a broad expanse of material, well-keyed plaster remains solid. Moderate water damage does not usually cause the plaster to come perilously loose or deteriorate severely.

Sweeney saw that the keying of the brown coat was still in good shape in most areas where plaster still hung. The "white coat," the thin gypsum outer coat which is then shaped smoothly to finish, was obviously going to have to be redone. The ceiling would be saved — rebuilt, restored. Myers was pleased. Sweeney agreed to send his report immediately and start negotiating a contract. "I went home happy that night," Myers says.

What if Sweeney had found the keying unsatisfactory? If what was left of the ceiling had been unsalvageable, it would all have had to be ripped out and redone from scratch. EYP had not yet decided on a fallback choice, and at that early stage the State Historic Preservation Office was following EYP's findings and recommendations. The initial application to SHPO said that the builders would "repair/replace" the ceiling plaster, either one, so long as the final appearance was in essence identical (including the color) to the original. SHPO in Albany, as well as Philadelphia, would surely want nothing less than a detailed accounting of any proposal to depart significantly from the original ceiling configuration.

In that first visit, Sweeney concentrated on the general ceiling situation. He only glanced at the prominent plaster ornaments: six cartouches[12] and the eight "Alexandrian" busts atop the arches. Inspection of those features could wait for his next trip to Albany, during which Dovetail would tackle the ceiling patterns, since they were the most pressing matter.

To replicate the ceiling, Dovetail needed to identify each of the design patterns visible in the ceiling. There were nearly twenty different repeat motifs, with colorful but accurately descriptive names like dentil, dart and egg, lamb's tongue, and acanthus leaf (the

pattern repeated in the cast-iron railings). Sweeney and crew came again in November. The plan was to saw out a sample pattern of each motif (in a length sufficient to catch the full recurrence of the pattern), take the piece to Lowell, create a mold around the cleaned-up and restored pattern, and produce whatever number of lightweight, fiberglass-reinforced plaster castings was needed to restore that pattern throughout the building. The production pieces (perhaps as many as two thousand of them) would be stacked up, like fine four-foot-long white panels, to await shipment to Norstar when the builders were ready to begin the installation.

The cartouches were something else. As plaster figures go, they were huge. Viewed from 50 feet below, it was difficult to appreciate that they were seven feet tall and weighed about half a ton each. In the absence of definitive records as to how they were installed in 1900, mystery still attended the medallions. They might have been built up from stock components ("You know," Sweeney smiles, "pineapples and griffins, your everyday sort of thing") available through catalogs from the many plaster shops then found in large cities, or they might have been cast as single pieces, at Union Station or elsewhere. Whatever their provenance, getting them down proved to be quite a challenge.

Sweeney chose to remove the one cartouche which was in the worst condition, ship it to Lowell, and replicate it. The idea was to attempt to repair the better-off pieces in place, while Dovetail would prepare backup castings in case the developers opted not to repair. During that November 1984 visit, Sweeney and two assistants went up in the "cherry picker"

Bob Sloan.                    Julie Stokes.

(similar to a telephone lineman's bucket on a boom) to spend a few hours chipping away at the edges of the piece and cut through the vertical metal supports running above and below it. Then they tugged it loose from its perch of eighty-four years and brought it slowly down to the ground. While the heavy, aging form settled to the floor, one of the three vertical metal brackets touched before the others . . .

The cartouche shattered into sixty or seventy pieces.

So they spent a few more hours moving shards around, photograph in hand, recomposing their Alexandrian Humpty Dumpty so that they could place it on a skid and hoist it into the truck. As his assistant bit her lip in perplexity, an unrecognizable chunk of plaster in her hands, Sweeney shook his head and sighed: "You're gonna do a lot of carving, kid."

In January 1985, Einhorn, Birdsey, Myers, Grey, and a new member of the team flew in one of Norstar's two planes to Connecticut to look at a similar ceiling restoration then in progress at the Richardsonian New Haven Station. The newcomer was Robert H. Sloan. Designated senior vice-president of Norstar and placed in charge of the renovation project, Bob Sloan would soon find his name linked in many minds with the making of Norstar Plaza. He became Peter Kiernan's man on the scene — every scene.

In a thoughtful but risky decision, Sloan had left the presidency of Albany International[13] after a thirty-four-year career there, announcing his resignation in July 1984 at age fifty-eight and shortly thereafter leaving "without a place to go the following Monday," he says. Kiernan soon contacted him. Sloan's business acumen, as evidenced in his work as president and CEO and, in 1983, his leadership of a $275 million leveraged buyout of Albany International, would be useful in Norstar's strategizing and investigating prospective financial-service-affiliate acquisitions (in addition to his supervision of the station project). Like Kiernan, Sloan was pleased with what he heard, too, and accepted. Perhaps he yearned once again for a good engineering challenge. He got a spectacular one at Union Station.

## CONCRETE AND STONE

Richard Quay and his brother Darwyn were co-owners of Clifford H. Quay & Sons, the Schenectady general contracting firm founded by their father in 1945. Masonry was their specialty. Although contracted initially to put in the tunnels beneath the DP facility, Quay & Sons would also cut the pockets in the brick walls, into which the ends of the new steel girders would be inserted. Additionally, of course, extensive flooring had to be poured, three elevator shafts had to be prepared, the existing brickwork had to be cleaned up where visible (inside mechanical workspaces and closets), and new concrete walls had to be erected in the north-wing, ground-level boiler room. Finally, Quay expected to fix up the two chimneys atop the south wing.

Quay & Sons began working in the early spring of 1985, at which time Cristo Demolition was still busy dismantling much of the interior. Cy Brownell, of Brownell Steel Co., Inc., and his workmen (all members of the International Association of Bridge, Structural and Ornamental Ironworkers, or Ironworkers Local 12 for short) were just getting started on cutting loose the galleries as well as the existing balcony and stair railings.

Once again Union Station was a busy place, this time with bulldozers and long-necked cranes running the show instead of locomotives and baggage carts. But Toni Cristo facetiously recalls one particular day when there was a palpable sense of rush and anticipation, the air positively electric with the excitement of people eager to get a ticket and impatient for the great moment. No, not the arrival of a train. "It was the day of the $44 million lottery," she laughs, "and everyone was scrambling to get lottery tickets. There was great camaraderie among the fellas of all the trades — people were shouting, 'Hey, let's see who wins so we'll know who we'll be working for on the next job!' "

Ed Grey, as always, was everywhere, keeping abreast of how the several jobs were proceeding simultaneously and where the problem areas were. One problem over which he had no control was climate. Although to most Albanians the winter of 1984-1985 seemed mild, it was cold enough for the construction workers, particularly the stone workers who were cleaning the exterior.

The station's granite façade was in remarkably good condition. Compared to the contractors working inside, Ganem Contracting of Clifton Park had little to do beyond tuck pointing the entire building — raking out the mortar between the stones and refilling with an industrial-strength caulking made of polyurethane which would protect against water seepage or breakage from freezing. (Time was tight, so Will Ganem and his men came back after the opening to recaulk all the coping stone joints.)

There was also some patching of holes and gouges, particularly a long scar around the rear of the station where a canopy had once mounted directly onto the granite (the front canopy was still in place, awaiting a decision on restoration). Ganem had to experiment with the texture and tone of the mortar, to mimic the appearance of the weathered granite. It was not an easy process. "Weathering made this a difficult building to *clean*," Ganem explains. "You don't want to clean the building too well, or it will lose its patina of age, which is one of its attractions." A mild restoration detergent got the dirt off without abrading the surface or affecting the mortar joints. Ganem's crew stopped at a certain stage: the finish looked clean enough.

Oh, yes: one small bit of stone work would wait until the end. The long granite nameplates on the front and rear of the building, which read, "New York Central & Hudson River Railroad," would be covered over with stone panels — removable, to satisfy historic preservation dictates — saying "Norstar Bancorp" and carrying the company's logo.

Finally, between the parking garage and the rear of Norstar Plaza there was more concrete work going on. Here a covered walkway and a terrace (for use in part by the cafeteria) were to integrate the two structures.[14] Architectural-quality concrete work was the province of the U. W. Marx Company of Troy. Similarly to Callanan, this firm was founded by a European, in 1950 by German-born Ulrich W. Marx. And like Doc Marcelle, Eric (as he's called) developed a personal, almost passionate attachment to the Union Station renovation.

Exterior stonework has
weathered the years very
well, requiring little more
than cleaning.

The name of the former owner
will not be effaced. Rather,
holes are carefully drilled to
allow installation . . .

. . . of the new owner's nameplates, front and rear, over the
original plates.

The canopied platform behind
the building now leads not to
the trains but to the bilevel
parking garage.

Such pride of craft is easily overlooked in something as seemingly utilitarian as concrete. Marx's project manager, Mark McClenahan, explained that architectural-quality concrete requires true creativity in fashioning the wooden forms for the pours. "They have to be quite intricate," he says, "to permit 'rustication' and resemble the stonework of the station's exterior walls." Furring (the placing of thin wood strips familiar to those who've taken plaster off old walls, from which comes an appealing texture), tinting, and sand-scouring: it's a deceptively subtle practice. In fact, McClenahan says, they went through three different pours over a 10-foot-high mock-up to find the right amount of pinkish tint — only to discover on the third try that surface preparation, and no pigment at all, produced granitelike concrete for Norstar Plaza's rear walls.

## CAST IRON AND STEEL

One of the highlights of Union Station, and one of the salient points on SHPO's list of preservation musts, was the splendid cast iron (produced, you'll recall, in an ironwork shop set up on site, in December 1899). The gallery façades were masterfully designed, simple yet sufficiently ornate to call attention to themselves. There were also long railings with beautiful curlicues atop the mezzanines. The same filigree graced the four balconies (two small and semicircular, two long and rounded on one end) which jutted out over the waiting room on the north and south walls, from whose lofty heights railroad officials could look out upon their crowds while the crowds might also be looking up, wondering who those men were and how they got up there.

Union Station's cast iron was visibly pitted from decades of neglect and years of exposure to moisture. (There were even places where the rails had been damaged by falling plaster.) Surprisingly, the extensive steel framing in the building was also corroded, rust having eaten away some of the mass of the beams (called "sectional loss"), thus weakening them. Although some steel columns and beams needed reinforcement, and a few pieces were removed, most of the structure could remain in place.

But before the new floor could be erected, the immense, two-story-tall cast-iron galleries had to be moved. From Einhorn Yaffee Prescott's drawings of where the galleries would be relocated, Tom Ryan and Chet Zaremba at Ryan-Biggs Associates PC of Troy, structural consultants to EYP, prepared detailed drawings showing how the galleries could be reattached and reassembled. Donald Brockwehl and others at MLB examined the structural drawings and readied the bid packages for the steel and cast-iron work.

As was mentioned earlier, the gallery job eventually went to Brownell Steel (to whom it was sublet by Schenectady Steel). Foreman Cy Brownell's thirty years' experience and reputation for ingenuity in such tasks was just what was needed, since the contract didn't specify how the galleries were to be relocated. Some engineers thought the façades would have to be completely disassembled (they were for the most part bolted, not welded, together, which at the time seemed fortunate). Others thought the galleries should be moved in large sections, to ensure they'd line up satisfactorily once they were relocated and reassembled. A few doubted they could be moved at all.

Before steel for the new floors
and widened mezzanines can rise
along one side of the lobby, the
cast-iron galleries must be cut,
removed, and stored along the
other side.

A five-ton, two-story-tall section
of cast-iron gallery is carefully
remounted on the new steel
structure, higher and closer to
the center of the interior than
in 1900.

Brownell finished his inspection and pondered. In the spirit of the developing Norstar Plaza tradition ("This is a fast-track job; we change the plans almost daily, whenever there's an unforeseen problem; how about we try *this*?"), he decided to start at one end and cut one fairly large piece loose from the iron mounts on the brick wall (it turned out most of the rusty bolts could not be undone and had to be burned off anyway) as a test of how long a section could be handled with the tall crane.

Simple. All he had to do was decide where to cut.

Brownell chose a small section first. The initial cut was at the first vertical column, amounting to one bay of the gallery about 15 feet long. At the northwest corner, they made their preparations, cut the last supports, and gently swung the piece around.

The crane operator estimated from his instruments that the piece weighed 5 to 6 tons. Some of that was debris trapped inside — bricks, coal dust (which burned during the cutting), even a telephone man's hammer, its label still legible. Still, they got it out, set it down next to the similar structure on the east side of the waiting room, and lashed it into place out of the way of the other trades and traffic. The whole operation — barely scratching the surface of the gallery work — had taken several days.

They got through the west gallery move with tolerable success. (Later, the east side would go much more easily by choosing to cut "wherever we figured we could reweld it," Brownell says. That way there would be a lot fewer pieces lying around needing reassembly.)

After the west-side gallery was removed, the ironworkers began erecting the expansive steel structure for the entire new level, one-half of the lobby at a time (as well as in the wings). After half of it was put up, the galleries were carefully hoisted again and swung into their new positions, one story higher and further in toward the centerline of the lobby. Meanwhile, three mammoth H-shaped beams were also being installed across the top of the south wing, part of the ingenious modifications for the board room.

An example of how the problems of fast-tracking showed up in wildly unexpected ways, often from afterthoughts, is evident in the steelwork. After all the steel had been installed and the framing contracts had been finished, the owner wished to add another elevator. At issue was allowing handicapped employees and visitors to reach the lobby conveniently. The elevator would have to be large enough to accommodate a wheelchair. It was not necessary to satisfy handicapped-access legal requirements, because a ramp on the north end of the building had been carefully planned to meet that need. But a new contract was issued and the work was done to accommodate those who could not negotiate the stairs and who might not want to take the long way around.

# The Shape

## ROOF AND FLOOR

The roof, curiously enough, had to be done first and last. It had to be constant protection for the interior, yet it had to be opened up regularly as a portal for many large pieces of equipment which could not be brought in any other way. Most of all, it had to be absolutely weathertight; there could be no repeat of the earlier destruction by dripping.

The 1900 roof had essentially been replaced by the 1979 OGS temporary roof, which was believed to be in fairly good condition, apart from a hole here and there. B. Sheber and Sons, the roofing contractor, sealed the holes in the OGS roof and mounted a steel deck and an inch-thick layer of insulating material; all this was designed to last a winter or two. Sheber then agreed to a 24-hour on-call arrangement because, as John Myers says, "We were constantly lowering something or other through a hole in the roof, and Sheber had to come in and patch up after us."

During the winter of 1985-86, Leonard Levine, president of B. Sheber and Sons, died. The resulting complications for the company obliged Norstar to contract out for completion of the repairs.

About this time, Bob Sloan recalls being up on the roof "with Ron [Norstar Plaza Facilities Manager Ronald H.] Noll and the architects. I noticed some blistered areas in the roof tar, as big as three feet in diameter. When I kicked them, I could hear water moving inside." At the next Monday morning meeting, Sloan came "loaded for bear." The team immediately began planning for a permanent roof.

The new contractor was Monahan and Loughlin of Glens Falls, north of Albany and Saratoga Springs. They put in a roof to end all need for roofs, essentially a huge rubber membrane in sheets measuring 40 feet by 100 feet. Coiled up, each was a 1,200 pound load for the crane delivering them up to the roof. The sheets were laid directly over the two temporary roofs, and a polyester protection mat was placed over the rubber mat. To keep everything from blowing away, 200 tons of stone (river-washed, with optimum smoothness and no sharp edges to poke the rubber membrane) were spread over the entire roof. Masonry-slab walkways were built to keep boots and the occasional dropped tool well away from the all-important rubber membrane. According to Monahan and Loughlin, the roof should need no maintenance at all.

The floor insertion was a job of similar magnitude. The new floor, which required construction of extensive steel framing; insertion of vast expanses of concrete; reattachment of the galleries; and installation of the fine marble covering, stretched the full length of the building. It's unfortunate that the skeleton of the new building must go unheralded, because the demands of the steel erection for new floors throughout the lobby, wings, and mezzanines were formidable. Consider the conditions:

> The building at that time was essentially at ambient temperature. As Toni Cristo says, "It was very cold when it was cold, and very hot when it was hot. At that stage of

The steel floor pans are going into place; soon the concrete will be poured for the new lobby level.

the job, nobody was going to take the time to make the place habitable."

The place was dirty and usually filled with a cloud of dust. Richard Quay says six of his men spent three months just cutting holes into the brick walls to accept the new steel beams; Cy Brownell recalls it was often so dusty that people didn't even try to talk.

Oddly, the interior was both dark and blindingly bright, with dozens of corners obscure save for temporary light while glaring sun poured in unfiltered through the tall arched windows.

Ed Grey and Bob Sloan feel that such uneven conditions may have contributed to a spectacular accident which spoiled an otherwise almost perfect safety record. On May 21, 1985, the steel erection for the new floors was under way following the removal of the west-side galleries. The long boom of a crane brushed from behind a 40-foot-tall column, part of the steel skeleton rising near the northwest corner of the lobby. It was barely a nudge, but enough to knock one end of a steel beam out of its wall pocket. The other end was being held to the column by an "erection bolt," a single high-strength bolt used temporarily at a plate which will eventually receive four or six bolts.

There was a banging noise, and things started moving.

Einhorn and Myers were walking outside the building in the rear, returning from lunch. They heard a resounding crash, as if someone had dropped a huge deck plate (which was a common enough sound during the project). They thought little of it, until they heard another heavy whanging, then another,

then several at once. Myers says this went on for probably 30 seconds, "but it seemed like three minutes. I remember thinking, 'It has to stop!'" As they approached the open side arch to look inside, a startled worker flew past, shouting, "There's people dead in there!"

All they could see was dust. Ironworkers shouted to one another the names of fellows unaccounted for. When the air cleared, Einhorn and Myers could see men clinging to twisted and drooping steel perches. As these people made it to safety and the area grew calm, everyone realized that, amazingly, only one man was slightly injured.

Sloan and the officials at Norstar felt great relief. They turned to the consequences of the accident, which, says Sloan, were "*much* less severe than we had feared at first. We were *very* lucky."[15] The steel structure would, however, have to be photographed in place for insurance purposes, inspected for safe access during the cleanup, partially dismantled, tested for invisible damage, and rebuilt. It might take weeks. It was the sort of delay that the project could little afford. Yet it was all done and work proceeded.

## WINDOW AND DOOR

The State Historic Preservation Office maintains a hierarchy of preferences on questions of permissible modification. The first preference is, always, to restore the original material and appearance.

Second best is to match replacement components or materials as closely as possible to the appearance of the original. The fall-back choice is to accept an alternative which might not match the appearance of the original but is a good-faith attempt to stay close to it.

The discussion of windows and doors illustrates this hierarchy. Most preferable for Stokes's office was to restore the original sashes and retain windows and doors identical to those of 1900. However, although the sash and framing that was still in place might have permitted some restoration, much original material was missing or irreparable. So the question became: aluminum windows or wood? Aluminum frames would be cheaper and could include custom extrusion, which would restore the exact outside appearance of the originals. But because the finish is baked on, the color would have to be the same inside and out.

Wood frames were more authentic; moreover, they could be painted appropriately inside and out, and builders felt quite comfortable about customizing to restore exterior appearance. Wood was the final choice. The Marvin Company of Minnesota, known for custom "monumental windows," manufactured the outside-facing windows and delivered them to the dealer, Quality Lumber and Builders Supply of West Seneca, near Buffalo. The installer was a local carpentry contractor, Paul Grow. The inside windows, such as those in the galleries, were crafted by Terminal Millwork of Albany (who also prepared the mahogany panel inserts in the façades). The hundreds of panes in the six arched windows were also upgraded, with a commercial "Add-A-Pane" system providing air-free insulation.

When it came to doors, the historic preservation priorities also prevailed. Norstar consented to having custom doors made, the three-panel style being used virtually throughout, in oak (by Quality Lumber) for the board room, anteroom, and Kiernan's office, and mahogany and poplar (both from Terminal) elsewhere.[16]

The owner and architect together insisted, however, on revolving doors as the main entrances. First, they told SHPO, to be efficient thermal barriers, hinged doors must be set into a vestibule of some sort. With the stairways of the redesigned entrance, there simply wasn't room for vestibules — unless SHPO wanted them to protrude outward and thus affect exterior appearance. A well-sealed revolving door, on the other hand, would provide effective climate control. Second, the Broadway entrance to the station had twelve tall but narrow (2' 10") doors, a set of four in each of the three window arches.[17] This was appropriate for a building into and out of which large numbers of people might simultaneously be passing, but unnecessary for the less trafficked holding-company offices. Besides, current building codes specified wider doors as main entrances. Third, the insulation argument was not trivial; people would be working just inside the doorways, in what could prove to be a drafty, unhealthy environment. In addition to comfort, the savings in heating and cooling costs would be appreciable with revolving doors. So maintained Norstar and EYP.

SHPO voiced the objection that revolving doors were a significant departure from the original design (to which the architect in turn pointed out the existence of revolving doors at the time Union Station was constructed). So it went; this particular dialogue continued longer than some others. There was no impasse, but still Norstar and EYP (and Kiernan and Sloan personally) had to invest time and preparation to mount the argument. At SHPO, Stokes, who had

been feeling out the reaction in Philadelphia to revolving doors, knew that in the final application the
alteration would be one more significant factor in
evaluating the entire project. The more give-and-
take now, and the more completely everyone could
document the reasons for proposing to change the
entrance doors, the better everyone's prospects for
success later. The revolving doors were eventually
approved and installed in late spring 1986.

## CHIMNEY AND CANOPY

There were other parts of the original structure which
were the subject of animated discussion with the State
Historic Preservation Office.

Two slim chimneys had stood atop the south wing
since 1900, erected for the kitchens in the station
restaurant. But Norstar Plaza would need chimneys,
or one chimney, only for its boiler room — which
would be in the *north* wing. All right, said SHPO,
realizing EYP could not relocate the boilers to the
south wing: you can fix up the two original chimneys
and create a third one, to look like the others, atop
the north wing. Wait a minute, said owner and architect; a costly and heavy new steel structure will have
to replace the brickwork of 1900, all to support two
nonfunctional chimneys. Wouldn't it make more sense
to tear down the chimneys and make one (or two) on
the north wing where it (they) would be functional?

The line of argument should by now sound familiar,
and the eventual resolution will have suggested itself.
The final decision: the two chimneys were carefully
photographed, dismantled (each granite block given a
number), and then reconstructed as one larger chimney atop the north wing. Thus it was "authentic,"
and functional, too.

The flue, it seemed, was not. Through a misreading
of a drawing, the dimensions of the chimney flue had
been made too small. The discrepancy was discovered
late, as the boiler plant was about to be hooked up to
get some heat into the place for the winter. Another
delay? Phone calls to the manufacturer of the boilers
confirmed that, even though smaller in internal dimensions, the flue could handle the load. No doubt
cheers went up; it was cold inside Norstar Plaza.

Then there was the front canopy. The early photos of
the station show an expanse of steel, cutting across
the three arched doorways on Broadway and extending fully 30 feet out from the building — in fact, just
over the curb of this main drag. Well, obviously
something had to give once the automobile (more
pertinently, the bus and the truck) took over Broadway. At some point early in the century, five feet had
been chopped off the front edge of the original canopy to clear passing vehicles — after the canopy had
already damaged a bus and a fish truck, according to
Sloan.

Kiernan and the Norstar people asked what purpose
a broad canopy would serve at an office building, in
light of the redesign and extensive rebuilding which
would be required. There was also the aesthetic question: the canopy visually broke the perspective of the
passer-by, who would not be able to see and appreciate the full height and splendor of the stonework.
And besides, the original canopy had stretched over
twelve entrance doors nestled in three archways along
most of the front of the building; it was meant for

lines of cabs drawn up at the curb throughout the day and night to serve thousands of travelers. None of this would apply to a corporate headquarters where two hundred some would enter once a day, mostly from automobiles parked in back.

Cristo Demolition awaited the go-ahead to dismantle what remained of the structure of the canopy. No go-ahead was forthcoming from SHPO. In one of her first meetings with Kiernan, Stokes had said that the front canopy was a significant design feature of the station, and a major exterior attribute at that. She then saw the project undergoing a string of modifications — inserted lobby floor; parking garage; relocated cast-iron galleries and chimneys; replacement windows; revolving doors — and now the owner was requesting an appreciable change to the exterior by removing the front canopy. In increments, the departures from conventional experience in adaptive-use historic renovation had reached the point where Stokes saw a real risk of Norstar's failing to get the investment tax credits (ITCs).[18]

In that event, Norstar would not be the only loser. New York SHPO had a lot on the line in this project, too. The negotiation process over Union Station/ Norstar Plaza was, nationally speaking, precedent-setting.[19] There was little guidance from past ITC cases. A great deal depended on the final-approval decision, as people all the way up to the Office of the Secretary of the Interior were aware.

Fully mindful of the consequences and with an eye on the importance of the project to New York State's role in defining a national stance on adaptive-use rehabilitations, Stokes felt that New York SHPO should accept the proposed removal of the canopy but advise Norstar that it was a risky choice. She urged submission of the request and supporting documentation so that Philadelphia could make the crucial decision.

If ever the stereotype of preservationist vs. owner came close to validity, it was in the debate over whether the front canopy would be retained. Both sides were adamant on making their points; both were reluctant to yield. When the answer came back from the Philadelphia office of Interior, it was not cursory approval: Part Two of the application was "marginally acceptable." SHPO, Norstar, and EYP had been probing the very limits of the permissible. Stokes sums up this difficult phase by saying that the three organizations had been "working out lines of communication, not lines of battle. We forged an alliance out of what could have ended up a no-win confrontation."

The controversial front canopy
initially extended fully over the
vehicles pulled up at the curb.
Signs on Broadway include
"XXth Century Lunch" and
"11 Barbers."

Antoinette Cristo (left center,
with beverage) and the demolition crew pose with freshly
liberated "Elvira."

## BUST AND FOUNTAIN

Those plaster busts visible atop the eight tall arches in the waiting room have been called everything from "Alexanders" to "Minervas" by the press and public. Gender aside, they are impressive works and quite large. But Bob Sweeney and John Myers discovered that, even though intact, the six busts along the east and west sides were not stably mounted on the walls. In fact, with the vibration set up by Cristo's demolition work the busts began to come off the walls entirely. So just before Sweeney's third visit, in March 1985 (once it was apparent that they could not be solidly anchored and rebuilt in place), one of the busts was brought down and made ready to be hauled off to Dovetail for replication.

Strict preservation would have required the retention of all eight busts. There would be no problem restoring the two busts over the end arches leading into the wings, as they would be far away from workstations and walkways. But once the new mezzanine levels were in place, it became clear that the six busts along the side windows would appear ridiculously large, out of all proportion to the workspaces to be just a few feet beneath them. The architects smiled at imagining a secretary at her desk, with a five-foot-tall Minerva head looking over her shoulder . . . .

To illustrate that point, one bust was temporarily hoisted into place for inspection by SHPO officials. Michael Lynch from that office readily concurred that the piece was wholly out of balance with the higher mezzanine level. He and Stokes then went to their superiors to tell them of the lengthy process thus far, relate this finding, and persuade them that it would not benefit the renovation to retain all the busts. Finally, the Philadelphia office agreed to require just the two over the end arches.

Where did the others go? Some are in storage. Toni Cristo kept one as a souvenir, saying, "During the demolition we got so attached to these ladies, or men, whatever they are, that we named them and treated them like friends. Mine is named Elvira." Authorities do not expect much demand in the future for authentic, but oversized, reproductions of Alexander, or Minerva, or Elvira, or whichever ones are still unclaimed.

Although most of the salient features of Union Station were preserved, there were some other victims in the renovation. One quasi-victim was the drinking fountain. As work got under way, a wide and shallow crescent-shaped basin of granite with a lion's-head spigot clung to the southwest corner of the waiting room. It survived, actually, though in a much less prominent location: outside Norstar Plaza, on the rear wall just to the left of the covered entrance from the parking garage. It's no longer operative.

# The Infrastructure

## HEATING AND COOLING

There was virtually no interface with the original fabric of Union Station in plumbing, heating, and electrical systems. Vandals had long since carried off anything usable or pawnable, even cast-iron lion's heads. Donald Hart, president of George Martin and Sons, the electrical contractor, says there was not a single original light bulb fixture left when they came in.

Very little piping was recyclable. Classic lead pipes are, of course, prohibited from use in modern potable water systems; not even lead-based solder is permissible. About the only material which had held up and not been carried off was the cast iron in the "risers," the vertical drains from the ceiling and upper areas (according to the chairman of plumbing contractor Tougher Industries, Donald McKay, in vertical applications cast iron may last "for centuries"). Thus the heating plant, air conditioning, and plumbing installations were, for those contractors, essentially equivalent to what they would have done on a new-construction project. Well, almost.

In June 1985, Martin, in a joint venture with a minority-owned business, Manila Electric, began the electrical work, while Joseph and Frank Campito started in on the heating, ventilation, and air-conditioning work (Frank recalled selling papers in the station as a youth). Those contractors came in just after plumber Tougher Industries (the company name is pronounced, says Chairman McKay, "with a Gaelic 'gh'"), a family-owned business whose founder was a nineteenth-century immigrant from Belfast.

The problem they faced was to insert a modern system into a 1900-era building. As drawn in the plans, a piping run might lead straight into 30 inches of brick. In a constricted space, work recently completed might have to be redone when it was discovered that something else just wouldn't fit anywhere else (Hart recalls on more than one occasion finishing something and redoing it "in the course of the same working day"). Yet, "considering the complexity of the entire job — ours and everyone else's —," says McKay, "we didn't have that many really awful surprises." Hart basically agrees, although he still shakes his head at the day-in day-out problem endemic in fast-tracking: "Changes, changes, changes."

Joe Campito identifies the one factor which kept the modifications and scheduling from becoming chaotic or ruinous: cooperation. He credits the architects and construction managers with "keeping on the pulse of the job"; when something was going wrong, they came over, listened, and went back to the drawing boards. "In a fast-track job, you can't design from scratch," observes Campito. "If you end up with a plumbing crisis, it's tough, because the walls are up — period."

The sheer scope of the installation on which these men were working is impressive. Two hefty gas-fired boilers (rated at 14 million BTUs/hr.) alternate 24-hour cycles. Two separate air-conditioning systems

The tape library, protected by an inert-gas fire extinguisher system, is part of the data processing facility now occupying what was the waiting-room floor.

Building Engineer Mike Plonka wears ear plugs when testing the diesel generator. The five conduits are the emergency electrical leads for Norstar Plaza.

cool the building generally and the DP facility specifically. More than two hundred fan-coil units on individual thermostats serve the offices, operating from two cooling towers, two 225-ton chillers, and three rooftop ventilation units.

## DATA PROCESSING

The computer facility is equally impressive. Once the decision had been made to dedicate the entire ground level to data processing, Norstar Services President Robert P. Drum and Senior Vice-President Robert J. Browne were given carte blanche to design a single-center processor literally from the ground up. Around the IBM 3090 Model 200 (which could be expanded to twice the speed and capacity with no further floor-space increase), they planned for 126 gigabytes of storage, hundreds of telecommunications channels for the banks and automated teller machines, 21 tape and 36 disk drives and controllers, the works. They placed the order on February 14, 1985 (three days after another green-light day, the approval of the Environmental Impact Statement). IBM acknowledged the order within the week and promised to deliver the system in 14 months.

The lead time seems amazing. But once the delivery date was definite, the entire Norstar Plaza project had to align itself around that target. If the computer were to arrive in April 1986, then the electrical systems, not to mention all the flooring, framing, mechanical, and furnishing/painting work in those spaces, had to be complete. Some fancy equipment would also have to be in place: Norstar was ordering a diesel generator, a UPS (uninterruptible power supply), and a set of batteries for backup power.[20] Downtime was a critical concern for the $11 billion holding company.

When Big Blue's mammoth, coolant-equipped tractor-trailer and three big vans arrived at Norstar Plaza's loading dock on April 25, 1986, Drum and Browne were ready. They had duplicated the *entire* installation still operating at 1450 Western Avenue, so as to be ready to switch over immediately. And during the Memorial Day weekend, they did it, in 23 hours.

"If ever we did anything right," Browne smiles, "that was it. We never had to invoke any contingency plans. We shocked ourselves. Of course, we had a helluva crew in here, with IBM folks coming in from all over New York and New England."

It's a $14 million system (excluding the diesel and related devices), watched over around-the-clock by nearly two hundred people. It's literally the heart of the company and its physical plant, very carefully guarded and protected against fire. Strangely, there are sprinklers installed above the computer cabinetry. Won't the computer cabinets get drenched? "Yes," says Browne. "But then IBM will come in and drain them. The cabinets generate enough heat that they'll pretty well dry themselves out. In most cases, we'd be able to power up within a few hours." And in the all-important tape library, where water damage could be catastrophic for the company, halon gas canisters will snuff out flames in seconds.

Norstar Plaza is just full of surprises.

## LIGHTING

The interior designers of 1900 gave Union Station a utilitarian lighting system by necessity, not choice. There was little theory of proper illumination of public or work places, not a great material selection, not even an alternative to incandescence. The world's first central electric-light power plant, in New York City, was only eighteen years old; fluorescent lighting would not make its appearance until 1933.

Early photos of the new station interior show what were called "electroliers" suspended 15 feet above the benches of the waiting room. Apart from those spartan chandeliers, light sources were scattered and dim. Far from the space-filling illumination we're accustomed to, Union Station's lighting was intended simply to break up the dark expanses of the interior.

In the first discussions of chandeliers, Kiernan mentioned the Rambusch Decorating Company of New York as a premier firm in historic-building restoration. It turned out they were also well known for custom lighting-fixture design. Paul Brasile, the lighting design specialist at Einhorn Yaffee Prescott, knew of someone else with an international reputation, William C. Lam of Cambridge, Mass., who had consulted on effective and efficient lighting practice in more than one thousand projects worldwide. Together Brasile, Lam, and Peter White at Rambusch shaped the system of lighting to accomplish two simultaneous goals: work well for office-task purposes, and enhance the beauty of the building.

Lam was not a stranger to Union Station; he recalled the building from his trip in 1941 from Honolulu to school in Boston. (He had also gone inside the empty building with Einhorn in the early eighties while in Albany doing the lighting for EYP's rehab of the Argus Building, their own offices.) Lam began by deciding to design new chandeliers, one for each of the nine ceiling coffers. There was no original design from which to depart, so he took his inspiration from Richardsonian chandeliers in various buildings around the northeast (they predated the Albany Union Station but were consistent with the work of his successor firm). An early premise was that the chandeliers would be hung high up, to highlight the ornate ceiling and to avoid breaking the sight lines at the mezzanine level. "At night," Lam says, "we should see glowing ceilings and walls." SHPO, too, wanted the passer-by to look in and see not rows of recessed light fixtures, but rather an unobstructed ceiling space and appropriate lighting units. Tom Birdsey of EYP comments that aside from the chandelier question "a big part of the conceptual problem was *integrating* the lighting, the infrastructure, and the overall design objectives."

As a general principle, Lam (working with Senior Associate Robert Osten in Cambridge) wanted elegance, something sympathetic to the idea of a railroad station. But more than that, Lam says, "I wanted to create the feeling of a banking house of the 1900 period," meaning he wanted to eliminate any sense of a cavernous ceiling above and beyond the conspicuous lights over travelers' heads. Lam was given plenty of latitude, according to Birdsey, who was the conduit for decisions on the lighting project: "Up to the point where SHPO would object strenuously, Lam was free to be creative."

Lam's "creative reuse project" started with specifying the size for the chandeliers, relative to the size of the ceiling coffers. He sketched the rough shape, to get the scale. As the design started to take shape, he considered some possible variations in terms of the arms, globes, and components; he would leave the final choice and detailed design to White at Rambusch.

Lam then moved on to his forte, technical questions of lighting performance and practicality — the choice of lamp source. The design work was picked up by White for the chandeliers and Brasile for most of the other lighting installations. There was indeed much to be done besides the attention-getting work on the chandeliers. Brasile was after solutions for highly divergent needs:

*Offices and corridors.* Lam's pioneering use of large-scale indirect lighting as the principal source of ambient light influenced designs for these low-ceilinged areas. The workspaces would be warm-lit[21] by fluorescent sources edge-mounted or clipped onto drop-soffits, to throw light up towards the ceiling of the office (the specific light could be chosen according to the palette of colors in each office). In the halls, linear fluorescent strips recessed into the overheads would form a long ring fully around each floor level. From outside the building, all lights should be unobtrusive and regular in location.

*Trees.* Plans called for potted ficus trees in the lobby. To highlight and nourish them, Lam specified narrow-beam halide fixtures, a high-intensity, cool-discharge source with good ultraviolet for plant biology. The nursery which would hold the maintenance contract

on the trees wanted at least 1000 watts for each one; Lam, Brasile and the Norstar/EYP chiefs thought that should be reduced.

*Low-ceilinged spaces.* In the south wing, where four floors replaced three, there was insufficient room vertically, and the space overhead was so packed that edge-mounted fluorescents just wouldn't fit. "This is a nightmare," Brasile said at one point; "there's too much infra and not enough structure!" Solution: the linear fluorescents were clipped directly onto the modular systems furniture.

*Exterior lights.* Lam was very sensitive to keeping exterior fixtures "invisible" to passers-by, saying that people should *see* that a building is lit but not *realize* that it is. Thus he gave Brasile some verbal instruction from which the designer took his lead and devised a clever solution. The four-globe lamppoles along the front of the building would support 500-watt quartz "wall-washers," one per pole, painted so as to be unnoticeable among the attractive globes.[22]

*Dimmers.* The final selection of incandescent, not fluorescent, sources for the nine chandeliers necessitated quite a few last-minute design changes for the electricians, including the use of dimmers on the chandeliers. There are four separate dimming systems in Norstar Plaza: the chandeliers and other lobby lights, the cafeteria, the conference/AV rooms, and the board room. Each is a "scene preset" system, which can be preset for a "cocktail scene" or a "slide-show scene," or whatever combination of dimmed and nondimmed lighting is desired for a particular purpose.

The decision to go with incandescent, not the high-efficiency fluorescent or the compromise compact-fluorescent, came about because a trial run with mock-up chandeliers (to be mentioned again in conjunction with the painting) showed that even the brighter compact-fluorescent didn't give enough light for the desired ceiling effect. Incandescents would definitely be costlier to run, but they could be dimmed, and that was important to full exploitation of the splendid ceiling and ornamental plaster. There would be a price for that effect, though: the dimming panel for the lobby system consumes as much as 54,000 watts.

There's more to fixing up a train station than buying lots of gray paint and lots of light bulbs. Details, considered each on its own, are important matters. Taken as a whole, they end up not inexpensive. But the details, skillfully selected and executed, contribute to the whole in ways which belie their seeming triviality. The lighting in Norstar Plaza makes that perfectly clear.

# The Finish

## PLASTER, PART 2

The higher reaches of the ceiling favored the replication approach since those motifs were clear to the artisans. When it came to the sections that were lower, Sweeney of Dovetail said, "We sometimes had to clean it up, because if man can reach it, man can paint it. Put forty coats of paint on and you lose the detail." Extensive areas had damaged surfaces or years of paint build-up; restoring detail would require considerable cleanup.

Now another problem loomed overhead: installation of the newly produced plaster castings. The matter had come up when Bob Sloan first met Bob Sweeney face-to-face at Dovetail in August 1985. How should the thousands of pieces be mounted, Sloan asked. The thought at the time was to have plasterers mount the castings and wet-plaster the missing areas, but Sloan and others were shocked at the estimates they'd seen for contracting such a job. Sweeney said he knew a couple of people whom Sloan could talk to. One of them was Ben Soep. Actually, Sloan had to go after him. Soep said he was very busy with a number of projects in Boston, felt he was working too hard and should slow down a bit, and thought that working in Albany posed a problem for anything but a consulting arrangement . . . .

But, he quickly added, the photographs of the station ceiling were alluring. Sloan knew what Soep wanted to hear (and see), so he offered to send the Norstar plane to Boston. Soep agreed to come take a firsthand look. "Well, really, I'm glad I did," he says in his droll but endearing fashion. "It looked . . . interesting."

He examined the specs for the job and began to formulate an approach which would give the desired results at reasonable cost. On another visit, over lunch at the Fort Orange Club in Albany, Soep told Sloan, Ron Noll, and McManus, Grey, and Dawsey of MLB that it would not work to have *plasterers* do the installation of the plaster castings — *carpenters* should do it. Eyebrows went up, and he was asked to explain. As he made his pitch, the consensus grew that Ben Soep was the man to put the plaster up. He begged to differ. He would gladly consult, he said, even take responsibility for the entire installation job, although he'd need a good foreman because he was already busy in Boston, and he was trying to slow down, he said, but boy, he sure had to admit those were some sensational moldings in that station . . . .

So Soep began the shuttle from Boston to Albany. "I wanted to do it because it was personally thrilling," he says, "to see the original work and envision how it was going to come out. With moldings like these, there was never any doubt it was going to be a masterpiece."

Thus it was that MLB's carpenters put up the plaster. Not wet gypsum, but drywall screws and wood compounds brought the castings together. A modest-sized scaffold on wheels allowed access to the ceiling without choking traffic on the lobby floor. Avoiding wet-plaster mounting had another significant benefit: it did not aggravate an already high moisture level in

Ben Soep.                                          Bob Sweeney.

the building (by February 1986 the boilers were running full-tilt, to dry out the interior following the spray-on fireproofing and to "heat the building and the outdoors," as Noll put it).

But the installation only *looked* simple. Every production piece was identical to the others from the same mold. However, the back of each individual piece had to be cut and scribed so as to fit snugly over whatever surface of bricks and metal brackets happened to be at the point of installation. More importantly, as Sloan points out, a 1900-era building was sure to have become out-of-square over time. Thus the plaster castings, although mini-mass-produced, were indeed hand-shaped for mounting. Soep commented at one point: "Compared to the original craftsmen, we've got a tough job here. Every piece has to join smoothly with the wall and with its neighbors. The final product must be seamless and appear regular to the eye scanning the length of the ceiling."

Handiwork extended also to the plasterers, who were asked to fill in the cracks where all the castings abutted, just as the old masters apparently had done in 1900. It took time, but it was delightful to do and see done. Things were humming.

Ben Soep on the job was just what one envisions for the anonymous foreman in 1900: directing traffic, coaxing and cajoling, shouting and sweet-talking. He imparted the fine art of decorative plastering, ran a trained hand over joints and seams, spoke articulately of eventual color choices and effects. He would brag about how well his fellows were applying his concepts, and then he'd mock-complain that they'd learned

it so well he had nothing more to teach them. He came in by 7:00 a.m. and said his cheery good mornings with a Bostonian accent as distinguished as his tailored shirts, fine ties, trimmed beard, and cocked hard hat. As with the other principal players in the Norstar Plaza story, Ben Soep left on his work and his co-workers an indelible imprint of personality and professionalism.

Soep got his "good foreman," too, in Charlie Kolber of MLB. Kolber had learned woodworking as an apprentice in the thirties on custom residential construction. He'd built airfields and hospitals in England and France during the war. Of course, he also built his own home. Affirming Soep's expectations, he utterly devoted himself to the job. In Norstar Plaza, Charlie Kolber *was* Ben Soep on the days when the restoration craftsman did not come over from Boston. He was the perfect intermediary for the odd pairing of skilled carpenters who were installing plaster castings and a painting consultant with a vision.

On January 24, 1986, Kolber ran busily up and down the full flight of stairs in Norstar Plaza "three or four times," he recalls, and then he didn't feel well. He eventually asked for the afternoon off and drove himself home. He was immediately hospitalized for a heart attack. Following five coronary by-passes (which, he asserts, are "a routine thing nowadays"), he squeezed his recuperation down to a mere month and headed back to work. Such was the dedication to the task which many people displayed, but which Charlie Kolber took to a remarkable extreme.

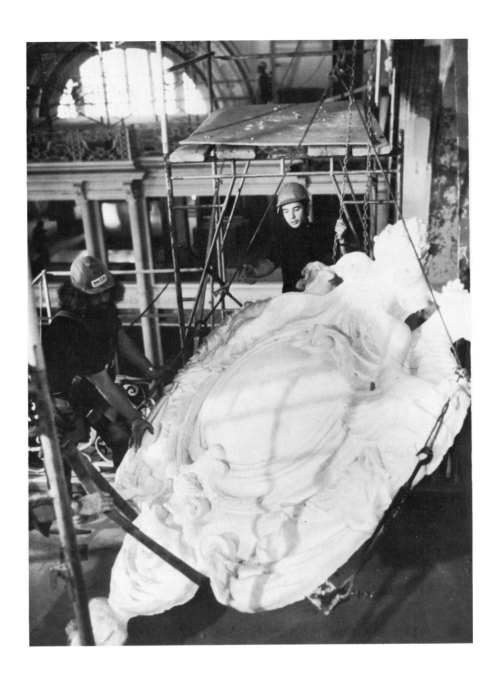

Up to its perch goes a cartouche,
freshly cast from the sample
which had shattered and then
been painstakingly reconstructed.

Carpenters install fresh plaster
castings amidst the darker originals, which are being restored
in place.

## PAINT

There was no greater question in everyone's mind than what the final interior would look like — specifically, what colors would be applied. Soep himself, rubbing his hands in anticipation, said, "Now we're coming to the most interesting part of the whole building, and that's the color." With SHPO's hierarchy of preferences (and the Tax Act Application) in mind, it was first necessary to determine what was original. EYP turned to Crown Restoration, a specialist painting firm near Ithaca, N.Y., to peel back the "forty coats of paint" that Sweeney had commented on. What would they find?

Plaster cuttings from the ceiling were carefully cleaned and the underlying layers of paint analyzed. The original paint scheme of Union Station: dark green and ochre.[23] The researchers then did up a sample plaster casting in those colors to show to everyone who would be involved in choosing colors.

The response was immediate and universal: the original colors were far too dark for the grand renovation of Norstar Plaza. Not the least reason was that people were going to be sitting and working just a few feet beneath that ceiling, up on the mezzanines. The oppressive color scheme seemed capable of driving someone to jump over the railing.

Well, then, how to come up with an acceptable alternative?

The owner and the architect approached William T. Weber at Rambusch in October 1985 to ask about the painting of Norstar Plaza. Back in 1979, Weber had corresponded with Paul Scoville, who was then preparing Einhorn Yaffee Prescott's *Historic Structure Report*.

Down in Greenwich Village, Weber put his best man to work on making some oversized watercolor sketches. Ronald "Buddy" Millard was a New Yorker who spoke like an Australian, having lived there for many years. He'd started as an apprentice at Rambusch and then studied at the School of Visual Arts in New York (where his father also taught apprentices). What followed was a sleeper of a craftsman's painting career: five years of night school; obligatory travels to Florence and the art centers of Europe; the Australian residency; and so on for thirty-three years with Rambusch, all the time doing murals and large-scale historic restorations.

Millard came to Norstar Plaza in early November to follow up on his sketches by doing a sample area of the southwest corner ceiling and part of a gallery. He was more than eager to talk with people about his concept, which for the ceiling focused on light and dark gray and slate blue, to evoke and complement the selection of black, white, and gray then being finalized for the marble floor. "There's a resurgence of true craftsmanship today," he said in his accented baritone. Millard, always meticulous, peeled tinsel-thin sheets of gold leaf and Dutch metal from pads as he spoke and, using a plain, dry paintbrush, coaxed the materials over and around plaster ornament. "It's happening just because people are now willing to do what is being done in this building. In some cases, it can be even less costly than a mass-production job with inferior materials."

A tireless worker, Millard threw himself into the sample sections at Norstar Plaza. The day came and the Kiernans, Sloan, Birdsey, Weber, and others inspected the proposed color scheme. The response was indeterminate, with uncertainty about the shade of blue and concern that there was too much gold trim. (Although people were there to appraise the plaster sample, Millard had also coated a portion of the galleries in white, more as a first step in masking the monotone of rusted brown than as any proposed coloration for the cast iron.) There was agreement that it would be helpful to see a larger sample.

There was also a consensus on the problem of lighting. For such inspections and high-level approvals, the enormous space, illuminated by temporary floods, was vulnerable to the level of daylight, which, on these November days, either streamed in or was nonexistent. "Colors were doing strange things," EYP Senior Designer Mary Whiteford says. "If you didn't like the looks of something at noon, you could come back at five and love it." Something needed to be done. As Millard left to go back to New York to work on changes, Leonard R. Fox, Norstar's building technical supervisor, was asked to create a mock-up of the chandelier design so as to get some appropriate and controllable lighting on the sample. Fox drove Millard to the Amtrak station across the river.

On November 23, Millard died of a heart attack in New York. What followed was a month of inactivity, during which circumstances began to demand that decisions be made promptly. At Rambusch, a search was on for someone free enough to pick up where Millard had left off. The delay, already significant, appeared insolvable, and Norstar, EYP, and MLB were all getting very nervous about the scheduling complications. Rambusch had given EYP not only an estimated budget but also a tentative timetable for

performance of the specialized work which their company proposed to do, and there were indications that accommodation to the fast-track process might be problematic. Meanwhile, in the course of a conversation or two at Norstar Plaza, an obvious answer to the problem presented itself. With his background, his familiarity, and his demonstrated capacity to work well with the principals on the job, Ben Soep seemed to be the ideal person to revise the sample paint scheme and perhaps go on to do the interior painting. Indeed, he approached Sloan and suggested that Norstar let him paint a test section.

He plunged in. After looking at the drawings for the marble floor and the chandeliers, he proposed focusing on warm grays, as many as eight shades across a spectrum ranging from glazed charcoal to bone white. Soep particularly needed the mock-up chandelier, to bathe the ceiling section in steady light of the sort which was going to be used in the lobby. He proposed doing a large section, from ceiling to floor, to let Kiernan and the others see the full splendor of his concept. That suggested preparing more than one mock-up, and so Fox and the MLB carpenters were soon in the chandelier-making business, with plywood, simple chain, gold spray paint, and inexpensive glass globes all over the floor at 1450 Western Avenue.

The cast-iron galleries were a real problem. The pocked finish of the cast iron, even after sandblasting, looked shabby with a monochrome coating, particularly a light tint. Soep had a secret weapon: his Polomyx, a "textured" paint in which black, gray, and white beadlets form a compound without dissolving into one another. He sprayed it the full height of the gallery section . . . and behold, the hitherto unsightly cast iron was transformed into a handsome, *stonelike* finish!

Soep in effect had revealed the unseen potential for making the cast iron a major part of the interior decoration scheme, rather than an incidental distraction. He recalls putting in a long night with test after test of golds over the textured gray, putting on gold and taking off gold, glaze in one place and leaf in another, applying a slow-drying second color over the gold and then wiping it off to leave a patina. He had a deep bag of tricks; he went way down into it, in search of just the right effect. He must have found it, because the reception of his sample, properly lit, from plaster ceiling down to cast-iron "stone columns," viewed from the far mezzanine and from the lobby floor, was impressive. With very little modification, it became the final paint scheme.

When Soep got the go-ahead to direct the painting as well as to finish up the plaster installation, he immediately recalled the name of a local commercial painting company, W. W. Patenaude Sons of Mechanicville, whose president, George Patenaude,[24] had already worked with Polomyx. Patenaude sent over two foremen, Ken Patenaude, Jr., and Larry Slocum, to work for Soep. The two were welcomed at the MLB trailer as the "experts" on Polomyx — although Slocum had never seen the stuff. Then Soep arrived, greeted them effusively, and talked to them at length, in his charismatic fashion, about the "concept" they were about to transform into reality. Slocum admits having been a little scared on that first day at the job. "And Ben never actually *told* us what exactly he did," he now chuckles. "It was quite a day."

Although Ken Patenaude was called away to run another job, Slocum stayed on. He gradually became aware of a change in his attitude toward his work. Soep, part mentor, part father figure, threw himself into the teaching of his own trade, and Slocum found himself responding in a way he'd never done, he says, as "just an industrial painter." The instructions became less minute as Slocum's competence manifested itself; the end-of-shift turnovers became less detailed, carried more responsibility. Within a few months, Larry Slocum found himself reappraising what had seemed a ho-hum trade. "This project, and working with Ben, opened my eyes," he reflects. "It changed me. It was an opportunity to prove to myself that I could be proud of my work — and that I could do whatever I wanted to do."

Slocum relished the greater responsibility George Patenaude gave him; they look forward to similarly challenging projects. He now thinks of himself as a true professional. He's another of the people for whom saving Union Station was a personally rewarding experience.

## BOARD ROOM

Fast-track planning, personal preferences, demands of elegance, and totally unforeseeable circumstances . . . these were the elements shaping Norstar Plaza. But in creating the board room, the mix was wilder than usual, affected as it was even by rain and international politics!

In the first discussions of what would be the bank holding company's most elegant space, Norstar management presented an amazing proposal: provide us with a room nearly 100 feet long, with no vertical columns. Realizing that this had to be done in a space whose height would be strictly limited, the architects were entitled to shake their heads. Were they being asked to design a board room, or a pizza carry-out box?

Kiernan, who had long admired the finely carved oak of the board room at the State Street offices of Norstar Bank of Upstate NY (the old State Bank of Albany building),[25] made a personal request: "I want the same feeling of that paneling reproduced in Norstar Plaza's board room." In this room, the board of directors would deliberate amid the finest of appointments. Thus there should be no protruding nail heads, no cut corners, no filler putty, no flaws.

First, the team agreed on the broad strokes. The 100-foot room was reduced to a mere 62 feet by 32 feet. Since the board room would be on the second floor, directly beneath the executive offices, the rearranged components of an original stairway could thus gracefully join these two distinctive areas. But no pillars?

Sure. Columns normally stand in *compression,* shouldering the weight of the floors above. Why not hang steel columns from girders in the attic? Then the columns, in *tension,* would *suspend* the third floor. The board room ceiling (that is, the actual floor of the executive offices above) would float above the room itself!

Three massive transfer girders were laid (by Stone Bridge Steel of Gansevoort) north-south across the attic of the south wing. From those girders descended H-sectioned hangers to hold up the floor of the executive offices. In the board room area, three vertical pillars were removed. Rusted steel was cleaned, tested, reinforced. The concrete floor was poured. Then, as if all this had not been challenging enough, the real troubles began.

*Paneling.* A laser beamed a perfectly horizontal line around the entire room, as a scribed benchmark for aligning ceiling and wall panels. And what a paneling job it was! Quality Lumber chose Eagle Plywood

and Door Manufacturing, Inc., in South Plainfield, N.J., to supply the veneer. White oak was sliced to $\frac{1}{32}$ inch, matched, and sequence-numbered to create "flitches," stacks of faces, one pair for each panel. To ensure uniformity of color and grain throughout, the veneers were then carefully inspected, selected, and designated for particular elevations in the room. Light-colored sapwood and defects such as knots were eliminated (only heartwood, about one-third of the selected veneer, was to grace these walls). Next, a sewing-machinelike stitcher joined each pair of veneers into a symmetrical face, which was then hot-pressed onto a particle-board core. After cooling, the boards were rough-trimmed, sanded, and shipped out. Quality Lumber then trimmed the panels to exacting order. Every measurement, in a room 62 feet long, had to be within $\frac{1}{16}$ inch. There could be no filling in of gaps; the panels must hang in perfect alignment on concealed clips. For consistent accuracy in mounting the clips, MLB's Carpenters' Supervisor, Clarence Conrad, passed around his personal tape measure (finally it was even shipped out to Quality!).

The grand opening was a month away. Where were the panels? They were coming, from Quality, but it was taking time to assemble veneer and solid oak stile-and-rail frames to the exacting measurements needed. It also took time to do the hand carving of the oak moldings which would run around the ceiling and doors. Quality's meticulous woodcarver could produce only two feet per day. At that rate it would take four months to finish these crown moldings and door casings and then match the pieces at each mitre and joint. Realizing that, Quality put extra staff on the job and turned up the wick.

*Flooring.* Concrete was poured, but measurements showed the floor was about one-half inch out of plumb. So the concrete was chipped out and the floor was resurfaced. Then high spots were ground down in preparation for the hardwood floor. But the traditional approach (concrete covered with a frame of two-by-fours and plywood, on which are laid eight-foot lengths of hardwood joined by tongue and groove) would not work; the architects could not spare even three inches of height in this long, low, chandeliered room. Visiting the Merchandise Mart in Chicago, Sloan, Einhorn, Whiteford, and EYP's head of interior studio Jim Dunlavey found James K. Moore, flooring expert. He gave them a tip: "Use shorts and mastic." Shorter lengths of hardwood glued directly to the concrete with rubbery mastic would also yield less movement with changes in temperature and humidity.

*Carpet.* Designer Classics in Waterloo, Ontario, got Norstar's order for a 56-foot oval of "designer velvet" in April 1986. Wayne S. Pauli, general sales manager, assumed responsibility for the job. He selected Scottish and New Zealand wool to be spun, dyed, hand-tufted, and, around the machine-made center, hand-sculpted. The final product on its latex backing would be a lush masterpiece weighing 100 ounces per square yard. It was shipped and stored in Albany until the board room would be ready, later in the summer, not long before the grand opening in mid-September. In August, when the thousand pound, 22-foot roll was hoisted through a window at Norstar Plaza and unrolled on the board room floor, everyone exclaimed in horror. It looked like an immense, soggy dishrag. The telltale rust of a shipper's forklift stained the sorry-looking tapestry. Somewhere it had gotten wet, been unloaded and unrolled in an attempt to dry

it out, and then carelessly rerolled. Following a frantic phone call from Norstar, Pauli, profusely apologetic (and furious), rushed to Albany. On his return, he put Designer Classics to work again on a fast-track replacement, starting over with extra staff on overtime. They had twenty-five days to go before the grand opening.

*Chandeliers.* Ordered locally, four handmade fixtures were about to be shipped from Barcelona, Spain, when President Reagan ordered the bombing of Libya on April 14-15, 1986. Following the raid, fear of terrorist reprisals obstructed commercial air shipments from Mediterranean countries; nothing was leaving Spain. "For weeks," recalls Ron Noll, "I avoided Peter and Bob Sloan and made a lot of calls. When the chandeliers finally arrived, I didn't take any chances. I took two fellows, and we drove to JFK Customs and grabbed them ourselves!"

Amazingly, all these pieces came together just in time.

When Jim Flury, Sr., the president of Quality Lumber, came to Albany with a party from his firm to see the building which he remembered as a dirty train station, he walked up to the board room area and was met by MLB's Conrad. The carpentry supervisor launched into such gushing praise on the quality of the paneling that the people with Flury thought the encounter had been staged to impress them!

Even the replacement carpet arrived in time. It was installed *three days* before the grand opening.

Hard-of-hearing board members were granted a personal request they'd quietly made, too. The chamber has been made noiseless (heating and air conditioning are silent). Moreover, wireless, battery-powered microphones beam the most softly spoken word to a hidden microwave receiver, which then amplifies the sound and feeds it to hi-fi speakers above the long mahogany table. Now everyone can conduct discussion . . . in splendid fashion.

## MARBLE

From the first, there was little doubt that Norstar Plaza would boast a fine floor of top-quality marble. The choice of quarry was also clear, a nearby firm with an international reputation for excellence and a history extending back to the mid-nineteenth century: Vermont Marble in Proctor, Vermont.

EYP Senior Designer Lucia Nyeu made detailed renderings of a floor design inspired in part by the pattern used by the original architects (Shepley, Rutan, and Coolidge's architects' drawings had turned up at the Fogg Museum at Harvard University) and, more apparently, by the arrangement of the coffered ceiling. From the renderings, three draftsmen at Vermont Marble could determine the scope of the work (16,400 square feet), after which everyone could move on to aesthetic considerations. In February 1985, Mr. and Mrs. Kiernan, Sloan, Einhorn, Birdsey, and Nyeu flew up to finalize the palette for the marble. There would be three colors: a white Royal Danby, a medium (Champlain) gray, and Champlain black, all from quarries which had been in operation since the early 1900s.

Sloan, Einhorn, Birdsey, and Harvey Vlahos (a filmmaker at Light & Power Productions of Scotia, N.Y., who was capturing highlights of the project on film) flew to Vermont on December 3, 1985, to meet Robert L. Tatko, the assistant general manager in Proctor, and check on the progress. The flight sticks in their memories because the plane[26] lost an engine on the return trip. After some anxious moments of "This can't be happening to us," the passengers were informed that the two pilots had chosen to land at nearby Glens Falls, N.Y. The landing, a tricky affair in wintry high winds on one engine, remains vivid to each of them.

As the date approached on which materials would start arriving, another architect from EYP, Timothy Cohan, joined Einhorn, Birdsey, and Myers to help coordinate communication between the fabricator and the installer, Hudson Valley Tile, a subcontractor who had removed the original granite wainscoting from the waiting room walls during the demolition phase.

Some four thousand pieces were produced, each cut to 1/32-inch accuracy, and each with a number on the back keying it to the detailed drawings of the new floor. The installation itself went very well — slowly, but exactly. Norstar was hoping to have the marble in place on the lobby floor for a luncheon on May 15, coinciding with the annual board meeting being held at the 1450 Western Avenue headquarters. By that date about 60 percent was in place; the work proceeded. To the credit of Hudson Valley Tile and the draftsmen and fabricators, the last of the four thousand pieces dropped perfectly into place.

# Color Plates

Still open in the fall of 1968,
Union Station betrays its neglect
as the end approaches.

The interior in 1984, as the
renovation begins.

Under a mock-up chandelier,
dozens of jobs proceed simultaneously in the fast track.

View from the south end of the
finished lobby.

The board room.

World-class fireworks over a
first-class renovation.

# The Sequel

## KINKS

Problems are sure to appear, considering the major surgery which this reincarnated 87-year-old has undergone. But it is the greatest possible praise for the builders' excellence that there have been remarkably few troubles, and only one of real importance.

*Marble.* As the September 1986 opening approached, the broad expanse of pristine marble spread finally to the edges of the lobby. Other jobs were still going on, though (finish painting, chandelier installation, even some last-minute iron and carpentry shop work), and workers and wheeled machines still needed to get around. To protect the new floor from scuffing or worse damage, it was completely covered with plastic. But under the plastic, grit was forced into the grouting and brushed across the face of the marble. The surface got pitted and discolored. After enough complaining from management, the fiberboard covering which had been specified in the first place was laid down. However, by the time the building had been open hardly a month, the luster was gone. In the fall of 1986, the entire floor had to be stripped and resealed.

Then little cracks appeared in some of the black marble. "Crack isn't even the right word," says Birdsey; "the lines are thinner than a fingernail — more like a crease in a piece of paper." Birdsey, Noll, and EYP's Steven Moulin surveyed every black piece and noted each one which had a pinch in the surface plane, some twenty-five or thirty pieces in all. In November 1987, Birdsey conducted another inspection; there's been no evident worsening. He feels the long thin sections of black marble are simply sensitive in one dimension to the slight movement of the building. But elsewhere, a couple of pieces of marble *have* actually cracked. It turns out they were laid across a nonuniform concrete joint. The workmen have simply refitted the joint and replaced the marble.

*Leaks.* The appearance of soggy plaster over the interior clock sounded another alarm. But what looked like a serious matter (a leak in the roof!) turned out to be less serious: water dripping from the flagpole.

The team sprang into action, for even a leaky flagpole could lead to serious consequences. They discovered the flagpole had not been constructed correctly, and moisture condensing inside it ran freely down and impregnated the ceiling plaster. That brought grimaces to the faces of everyone who had seen the original ceiling of Union Station after the cumulative effects of what had begun as just such minor dripping. The flagpole was fixed properly.

The infrastructure has proved somewhat more cantankerous. In grafting high-tech musculature onto some fairly old bones, points of rejection were bound to exist. The boilers have sprung several leaks, as have some of the plumbing joints up in the attic where 200-foot-long piping runs expand and contract. The solution for the joints was to install catch pans with small floats hooked to high-level alarms. The attic in Norstar Plaza is now an unseen delight: with these ingenious pans beneath neatly labeled pipes

Four thousand pieces of marble
were laid so meticulously that
only the tiniest of cracks would
later appear.

("CHILLED WATER ⟶ ") crisscrossing the rough-hewn giant anthills of the ceiling coffers, it looks like a cinematic ocean liner constructed from papier-mâché sets.

*Revolving doors.* Then it was noticed that no one was using the revolving doors. People were instead using the hinged doors which flank the expensive thermal-barrier revolving doors. Norstar officials discovered the reason themselves: the doors were too tight. So the rubber lips on the bottom edges of both doors were shortened slightly and the doors have become the principal conduits they were intended to be.

*Fire alarms.* Then there were the fire alarms. From day one, they lent episodic drama. The daily hum would be shattered by a shrill alarm, and then the Albany Fire Department would roar up. Or at least the Albany Fire Department roared up the first three or five or ten times. After that, as the exasperating condition continued for weeks and months, the response time understandably began slipping.

This was dangerous, of course, having the computerized alarm system continually shouting wolf.[27] Investigation turned up several causes for alarms: relays that malfunctioned; smoke detectors that were triggered by, say, a cloud of dust rising from the dumpster in the trash room; and so on. But the worst culprits were faulty smoke detectors, so sensitive that they could be set off even by the trace particulates from the butane-powered buffer which is prescribed for use in polishing the marble floor. Each time an alarm sounded, of course, the unit betrayed itself on the computer printout and was promptly replaced. Nevertheless, the problem continued for a full year before the false alarms became a memory — well, almost: during a party held in the lobby, a helium-filled balloon got loose, rose, and broke the infrared beam of the smoke detectors, causing a startling interruption of the party. Since then, use of balloons has been firmly discouraged.

KUDOS

Words — and works — of praise have proliferated around Norstar Plaza.

The adaptive-use historic renovation has won an impressive list of awards (all but one in 1987):

> *EXCELLENCE IN DESIGN AWARD*/New York State Association of Architects/ American Institute of Architects.
>
> *HISTORIC PRESERVATION HONOR AWARD*/National Trust for Historic Preservation.
>
> *RECONSTRUCTION PROJECT AWARD*/ *Building Design and Construction.*
>
> *GRAND AWARD FOR BEST COMMERCIAL REHABILITATION PROJECT*/Builder's Choice, *Builder.*
>
> *REMODELING DESIGNER OF THE YEAR, FIRST PLACE, RESTORATION/PRESERVATION CATEGORY*/Qualified Remodeler, Inc., *Commercial Renovation.*
>
> *HONOR AWARD*/Capital District Masonry Institute.
>
> *EDWIN F. GUTH MEMORIAL AWARD OF MERIT*/Illuminating Engineering Society.
>
> *TUCKER AWARD FOR ARCHITECTURAL EXCELLENCE*/Building Stone Institute.

*GRAND AWARD FOR ENGINEERING EXCELLENCE*/American Consulting Engineers Council, *Civil Engineering.*

*HONOR AWARD FOR ENGINEERING EXCELLENCE*/American Consulting Engineers Council of New York State.

*PRESERVATION MERIT AWARD*/Historic Albany Foundation.

*AWARD OF EXCELLENCE*/Architectural Woodwork Institute (1986).

*GRAND AWARD*/Renaissance 87 Design Awards, *Remodeling Magazine.*

*BEST PROJECT AWARD*/Bricklayers and Allied Craftsmen.

Norstar Plaza has also elicited the one thing which speaks louder than words. Although it was not the first rehabilitation in the downtown area, for many a development-minded person the announcement on April 11, 1984, was a watershed. It turned latent interest into active commitment, to the benefit of the entire city and citizenry. The buildings and lots visible in a semicircle around the front side of Norstar Plaza have almost all been renovated or earmarked for development since 1984. They include several buildings whose historical importance was forgotten, such as the former residences of Governor De Witt Clinton and Albany Mayor Abraham Yates (ca. 1790); a building dating to 1852; and the venerable Kennedy Garage.[28]

Surrounded by all this rehabilitation is Tricentennial Park, the centerpiece of the project's public/private collaboration with the City of Albany. With the exception of Norstar Bancorp's provision of four lampposts, some trees, and a fine statue, the city gets and

deserves credit for the creation and construction of Tricentennial Park. The statue which Norstar commissioned and donated is an exactingly done bronze of the seal of the city by cartoonist and illustrator Hy Rosen.

TOASTS

There was no shortage of well-earned celebration following completion of the building. Even earlier, on September 30, 1985, Norstar had invited the media to an on-site progress report, at which Kiernan and Whalen acknowledged the work and spirit of the builders of Norstar Plaza at a luncheon. All workers were given Norstar Plaza jackets and their pick of photos of themselves at work around the site. Now, in September 1986, it was time to let the whole city celebrate.

Thursday, September 18: Norstar held two receptions for its employees and their families inside Norstar Plaza. The cast and band of Up With People, 130 youths from eighteen countries, performed excerpts from their touring show, as they'd done at an unprecedented three NFL Super Bowl games. The 700 guests also viewed the lively 16-minute film which Harvey Vlahos and Light & Power had done for Norstar,[29] and toured the completely renovated interior.

Friday, September 19: A cloudy day finally broke, and a reported crowd of 100,000 people came downtown to celebrate the public opening of Norstar Plaza and Tricentennial Park. Governor Cuomo, Mayor Whalen, Kiernan, and others spoke at the dedication of the park, and Up With People performed again out in the park, to live television news coverage. The festivities then moved to the waterfront Corning Preserve, where the crowd enjoyed food, refreshments, and live music from the zoot-suited New York City Swing and the nattily uniformed United States Navy Band and Chorus.

Inside, a reception was held for the dignitaries who had dedicated the park and officers and directors associated with the Norstar company, along with their families. Up With People gave their fourth performance in two days for the 256 guests, who then moved out to the upper deck of the parking garage. There, the Norstar guests and the frolicking crowd in Corning Preserve watched a laser show by Image Engineering of Boston (with computer-controlled laser images cast upon the rear side of Norstar Plaza in synchronization with a local radio station's live broadcast). The finale for the evening: Albany's first-ever world-class fireworks by the famed Grucci family, the computerized pyrotechnics being launched from barges in the Hudson River. The Norstar party went back inside and gradually closed to the music of the Albany Jazz Ensemble.

Saturday, September 20: a black-tie dinner for 216 people at Norstar Plaza, with music by Lester Lanin and his orchestra.

Sunday, September 21: open-house tours for the general public. Long before the 2:30 convening time, people were lining up on Broadway for their first look at the renovated interior. An astonishing 10,000 visitors filed into the building that first Sunday. The short version of the film was shown continuously in the conference room, while students from Siena College, thoroughly trained for the occasion, guided the groups around the lobby, up to the board room, and

back, answering countless questions from rapt spectators. (Earlier that day, Norstar Bank of Upstate NY had held tours and shown the film to its employees and their guests.)

Sunday, September 28: Several thousand people endured heavy rains for the public tours. That morning, Norstar had hosted a reception for the builders, craftsmen, and artisans and their families and guests,[30] with tours and film. (It's easy to imagine how enthusiastically the question-and-answer sessions must have gone with *that* group of people there to point and explain and boast.)

The work necessary to bring off that program of events was itself staggering. The opening festivities were, organizationally speaking, a microcosm of the entire renovation project. Though inexact, the parallel to the Norstar/EYP/MLB collaboration was Norstar's Corporate Communications department (then headed by Barry Brandt) working feverishly with Light & Power Productions, under the direction of Chuck Hanley and John Deitz. Brandt's and L&P's staffs — on a fast-track schedule of their own — planned, procured, and policed everything from entertainment contracts, barge rentals, and security to swizzle sticks, custom chocolates, and motorbikes. What Bob Sloan was to the renovation project, Joyce Flanagan, Norstar's public relations assistant, was to the opening. She showed up everywhere, found everything, and helped everybody.

That week in September 1986 was a perfect public celebration of an extraordinary accomplishment. It was a generous, tremendously successful wrap-up to a 21-month, $20 million project[31] which put hundreds of area builders to work for 50-some subcontractors and brought a host of benefits (material, financial, and spiritual) to a population and regional economy lying well beyond the immediate neighborhood of what had, not long before, been called an eyesore, Albany's albatross.

Union Station was long a source of pride for its community, though surely few people claim that about the years of declining ridership and physical neglect. When all the hoopla had quieted down, there were occasional whispers of displeasure. Some people wanted *Union Station* to emerge from behind the scaffolding, not Norstar Plaza. One of the September visitors, in his eighties, revealed that sentiment while on a public tour, as he looked around, sniffed, and said, "It's nice, but it's not a train station."

To such criticism, Julie Stokes, as guardian of the past, has a thoughtful response. This was an adaptive-use renovation, not a restoration. In real terms, where would the impetus, the direction, and the resources have come from to restore this immense train station?

Stokes as much as anyone wanted the project to succeed. "Norstar's willingness to see it through to completion was never in doubt," she says, and when it became obvious that the owner had no intention of cheapening the end result, the terms of battle, so to speak, relaxed. "There was some degree of fighting on many issues," Stokes recalls. "All right, every issue, let's say. But we understood that we were fighting *with* them. Not everybody will like a given renovation. But how many grand buildings will survive at all?"

"The bottom line?" Stokes concludes, "Union Station is still there, and the people of its hometown can look at it with absolute pride, even if not with unanimous satisfaction."

## TIME CAPSULES

The Mayor and his fellow dignitaries interred a time capsule, intended for Albany's 400th anniversary in 2086, behind the Hy Rosen statue in Tricentennial Park on dedication day. The items in the capsule (most ideas submitted by Albany residents in a contest) included a program from the First Church in Albany, formed in 1642; a copy of William Kennedy's *O Albany!*; a panoramic photo of the city's skyline; and strategic plans for the city, to be examined a century hence. Tricentennial Commission Chairman Lewis A. Swyer presided over the interment of the capsule, with media reportage and other steps being taken to ensure that celebrants at the 400th birthday would know where to look for this gift from their past.

There was no such treasure map for another time capsule which surfaced during the partial demolition of Union Station. An employee of Cristo Demolition, Michael A. Adair, was "pounding away" at one of the badly deteriorated cartouches with a 16-ounce hammer when he noticed something inside the casting. He had barely missed smashing a glass bottle . . . with a handwritten letter inside! Adair took the bottle home, unopened, as a souvenir. But his conscience ultimately prevailed, and he decided to bring the bottle to Norstar. The letter was uncorked from the bottle at a press-conference/ceremony on January 22, 1987, at Norstar Plaza. Kiernan and Whalen looked on as Len Fox[32] retrieved the letter and handed it to the Mayor.

"Albany, N.Y., August 12th, 1900," the Mayor read, and the thrill of hearing themselves addressed from eighty-six years past was palpable among the listeners. The Mayor continued:

The Broadway clock has been reconstructed around the original numerals, the sole surviving components, found in the attic.

This Depot was Plastered by Smith and Eastman of Chicago Ills. A.A. Johnsen had full charge and started April 14th 1900 and finished August 15th 1900. The Ornaments was made in the Building. These Shields was put in Place by T.E. Fitzpatrick, James Sheahan & James McGill of N.Y. We worked 8 hours a day and wages was 45 cents per Hour. Double time for overtime during July and August we worked three Hours. Overtime also Sundays to Conplete [sic] the job on time.

Shepley Rutan & Coolidge of Boston was the Architect. Norcross Bros. done the mason work. On the other Side is the names of the Plasterers that was on the job at the finish.

[over]

A.A. Johnsen, Matt Carroll, T.E. Fitzpatrick, Andrew Johnsen, Fred Groth, Alex Garden, Walter Crimp, J. Taylor, James Sheahan, John Figgins, James McGill, Paul Klopsoh, John Andrews, Si Bartolomal, Will Andrews, James Gourlay, George Reed, A. Corcoran, Thomas Ennas, Harry Merriman, Thomas Patten, Walter Bogel, Ed Davies, Pat Mulhare

Paul Klopsoh and Si Bartolomal done the Casting for the job.

A.A. Johnsen Foreman August 12th 1900

There was clearly as much pride-in-workmanship crafting Union Station in 1900 as there was at making Norstar Plaza in 1986.

The letter has been preserved and is visible in the board room.

Two good time capsules deserve another. Norstar then placed a new one, a safe deposit box, behind the cartouche on the northeast corner of the interior. In it are lists of those who participated directly in the renovation, Bancorp employees at the time, all five issues of the *Norstar Plaza News* and the *Visitor's Guide to Norstar Plaza,* one of the key-chain mementos given to the builders, and fact sheets on the company and the new building. The English was much improved over that in the letter from A. A. Johnsen, but the spirit was little changed.

The press and media shot pictures, asked questions, chatted, and, before leaving, took one more look around at the splendor of the renovated interior. The Norstar staff went back to work. The building, no less a personage in this story than its people, hummed and whooshed softly, doing what it set out to do after a group of craftsmen and laborers, way back in 1900, finished off a bottle of who-knows-what, carefully scrolled a simple greeting to posterity, and went back to their own work, a little prouder than before.

# Notes

1. Matthew Josephson, *The Robber Barons: The Great American Capitalists 1861-1901* (New York, 1934), 191.

2. Boston architects Shepley, Rutan, and Coolidge were the successor firm to the great Henry Hobson Richardson. Richardson designed Albany City Hall and collaborated on the New York State Capitol, which was, in 1898, the most expensive building in the United States. Largely on the merits of the successor company's creation of South Station and the prestige of their Richardsonian legacy, Shepley, Rutan, and Coolidge were chosen by the New York Central & Hudson River Railroad to design Albany's new depot.

3. Coincidentally, formation of the new holding company was approved at shareholder meetings held on November 8, 1971, the same day that the State first attempted to auction off the granite white elephant which ultimately became the company's splendid headquarters.

4. The architectural firm was called Einhorn Yaffee Prescott & Krouner PC at the time of the April press conference. By the end of 1984 the present name was in effect.

5. According to Stokes, the fact that the building was still owned by New York State's Office of General Services gave SHPO jurisdiction. Certain federal historic-preservation guidelines and rehab regulations (for example, the requirement to produce an environmental impact statement) would be invoked for other reasons as well, including any application for urban development grant funds. Stokes clarified that electing to apply for investment tax credits had as a consequence compliance with the highest standards of historic-preservation work.

6. The transcribed minutes of the public hearing on the "Union Station Land Use Improvement Project," held on July 11, 1984, at City Hall, show that no objection was voiced at all:

> *PUBLIC HEARING OFFICER:* I would entertain any public officials or any members of the general public who might wish to comment on the proceedings thus far this evening.
>
> (No response.)
>
> *PUBLIC HEARING OFFICER:* Hearing none, the public hearing on the project is adjourned at 7:07.

(Transcription courtesy Joseph Stellato, Director of Land Utilization, OGS)

7. The National Flood Insurance Program (part of HUD) makes information available as to how high water is known to have risen during floods within the last 100 and 500 years at the site in question. This knowledge would have significant bearing on plans to erect new foundations. Norstar's data processing managers found the information interesting, too, since their computers would be in the lowest level of the building.

8. It also reminds us that in that time a visitor to the settlement "could at once see what kind of blood ran in their veins, for they either fixed exorbitant prices for their services or were very reluctant to assist me. No one goes to Albany without the most pressing necessity due to the avarice dwelling there." (The EIS cites "Colonial Albany," an unpublished dissertation by S. E. Sales, 1973.)

9. In an interesting coincidence, Hiser and Einhorn were both at the Syracuse University architecture school but had not met.

10. One of Norstar's principal objectives in selecting subcontractors was to surpass the quotas for women and minority hiring and subcontracting. The quotas were mandated by the legislative obligations which came bundled with the federal funding. Cristo Demolition, Inc., was the first of several WBE/MBEs (woman- or minority-owned business enterprises) to work on Norstar Plaza. Ultimately, all but the most stringent set of targets were exceeded.

11. The work was completed by another qualified asbestos remover, T. J. Bell of Albany, with the help of Cristo Demolition where appropriate.

12. There were originally eight cartouches in the interior, two on each end wall and one between each pair of side window arches. Vandals early on had stolen the copper flashings from the edges of the roof, and so water running off the sloped centerline of the roof eventually poured down the side walls of the interior and destroyed much plaster, including the two cartouches on the west side wall. As the Norstar Plaza renovation got under way, the two on the east side were still in place, though badly decomposed.

13. Founded in 1895 as Albany Felt, it is the world's leading producer of the special belts used in the paper-making process.

14. A small addition to the northeast corner was to house the mechanical rooms: the diesel generator and related power equipment, the cooling towers, trash facility, and loading dock.

15. The only other significant accident on the project occurred as a beam was being winched down into an elevator pit. The gears got disengaged and the beam fell a short distance, striking the foot of an ironworker. He was hospitalized with fractured and dislocated toes. Apart from these two minor personal injuries, the Norstar Plaza project safety record was characterized by Sloan as "excellent."

16. The visitor to Norstar Plaza can see two of the original doors of Union Station displayed in the recessed (and nonfunctional) doorways labeled "Offices" to the left and the right of the Broadway façade's three arched windows. The fine bevel trim is authentic.

17. Apparently around 1917, the New York Central filled in alcoves to create a mezzanine and installed ticket counters along the west gallery (the Broadway side) of the waiting room, thus closing off the center of the three sets of narrow entrance doors.

18. The Tax Act Application was a three-stage document. In Part One, SHPO and the owner/architect demonstrated that the building was of historic value. In Part Two, Norstar described plans for the rehabilitation, specified all modifications, and agreed, among other points, to the complete replication of all eight plaster busts (see the following section) and the repainting of the ceiling in its original colors (at that time still unidentified). It was acceptance of Part Two of the application which at this point concerned Stokes and the other principals in the project. Part Three, which would follow completion of the renovation, amounted to the request for final approval by the Department of the Interior and the granting of the ITCs.

19. Norstar Plaza appears to be the only major passenger station building in the U. S. which has been adapted for use by a single private-sector owner.

20. This expensive and complicated installation has earned its keep. With a computer system of this kind, even a surge or dip in power, not to mention an outage, can lead to a shutdown. In fact, according to Browne, following the start-up at Norstar Plaza there have been at least sixteen "sufficient blips" or power outages which would have necessitated calling in IBM to get the system up again, reload memory, and restore operation. This very time-consuming process has been avoided each time, as the battery backups have kicked in. If commercial power goes out for fifteen seconds, the V-12 Caterpillar diesel starts up and Norstar Plaza continues on its own power (with vital loads being the DP facility, emergency lights, and one elevator).

21. The color of fluorescent (and incandescent) lights is described by designers in terms of the equivalent temperature at which the source operates. Warmness is the inverse of actual temperature, such that warm white equates to a black body of some metal being heated to, say, 2800° Kelvin, while a "cooler" light might be rated at 4000°. By comparison, daylight is around 6000° — positively chilly, even on a scorcher of a day!

22. The poles and bases, of cast iron for longevity, match those at another redevelopment location in Albany, the Pastures. The arms are aluminum.

23. Contemporary accounts of the new Station came tantalizingly close to relating this information, without really saying what the colors were. *The Railway and Engineering Review* of March 16, 1901, says the walls were "plastered and tinted with kalsomine [calcimine] in color." The cast-iron galleries, according to the magazine, are "tinted a verdigris color," presumably a lighter shade than the dark green which the railroad always had in surplus and readily used later on to "brighten" things up. Perhaps not so surprisingly in a publication of a distinctly engineering focus, but disappointing nonetheless, the article makes no mention whatsoever of the ornate coffered ceiling or its decoration.

24. Of eleven Patenaude children and four stepbrothers, eight were active in the family business when their father, Wilfred, who had founded the concern in 1930, died in 1972.

25. The building, at 69 State Street, today still boasts the original façade of Philip Hooker's 1804 bank building. During the construction of the State Bank "skyscraper" from 1927 to 1930, the

façade was taken off the humble structure and moved, well-packed and on rails, about 50 feet to become the main entrance of the rising office building.

26. The particular plane was not one of Norstar's two aircraft, but a chartered twin-engine which had been substituted for an unavailable Norstar plane. Sloan says the episode made him grateful for Kiernan's earlier decision that the company would always use twin-engine aircraft.

27. There's a hidden danger in frequent false alarms: on each one, the normally closed exterior fire doors in both wings are forcibly opened and the huge suction fans in the attic kick in to pull smoke away. "Someone standing unawares by one of those doors could get hurt," Sloan remarked. The sequence is also expensive, since the air conditioning/heating system then takes hours to recover temperature control.

28. To preserve a story too good to pass into oblivion, Norstar's Len Fox remembers being recruited into the Army in the Kennedy Garage building. The inductees were told they would have their last civilian meal in the celebrated Rain-Bo Room of the fine Kenmore Hotel around the corner on North Pearl. Fox and fellow recruits marched up Columbia Street, through the revolving door, into the kitchen — and right back out, "orders to go," of an entirely unexpected sort, in hand!

29. The promotional film, shot in 16mm, was named the best community relations film at the 1987 Film Festival of the Public Relations Society of America. Vlahos also produced, shot, and directed for Light & Power a 28-minute documentary film for public television distribution, "Portrait of a Landmark: Union Station Reborn." This film was aired five times in the Capital District following the opening of the building and has been shown elsewhere on cable and educational television networks. Both films are available in VHS videocassette or 16mm motion-picture format by contacting Fleet/Norstar Financial Group, Inc. (the company's new name as of January 1, 1988), at One Norstar Plaza, Albany, NY 12207, tel. (518) 447-4401.

30. Bob Sweeney and his wife, Judie, attended. On March 23, 1986, a disastrous fire — which burned for a week — had destroyed Dovetail (the "Sweeney Building" as it was known to residents of Lowell) and a number of other buildings. Dovetail, Inc., is in limbo, with neither staff nor shop. Sweeney is now living in Peru, Vt.

31. The figure does not include those costs incidental to or independent of the actual building renovation (items as disparate as the DP center's new computer system and expansion furniture for departments which were previously renting furnishings). From the $20 million figure should be deducted the 25 percent historic tax credit — successfully obtained following SHPO's final certification inspection. Sloan sees the square-foot cost of $150 as "not unreasonable for a showcase headquarters important to the image of the banking company."

32. Fox was chosen to open the bottle since he is the first-ward alderman in Albany and the 1900-era artifact was imprinted with the stamp of the bottle's maker, James J. McGraw, who was then the city's second-ward alderman.

# Index

*Book Design:* Diana S. Waite, Mount Ida Press, Troy, New York
*Cover Design:* Stephanie Friedrich Fisher, Albany, New York
*Typography:* The Letter Shop, Albany, New York
*Printing:* Crest Litho, Watervliet, New York

*Photo Credits:* Donna Abbott for the author, 29 left, 30, 46, 68. Donna Abbott for Fleet/Norstar Financial Group, 49, 50, 51, 52, 54, 55, 58, 64, 74, 76, 77, 88, 89, 90, 94, 99. Donna Abbott, courtesy *Capital District Business Review,* 29 right. McKinney Library of the Albany Institute of History and Art, 9. Einhorn Yaffee Prescott PC, 11, 12, 34, 38, 87. *Railway and Engineering Review,* March 16, 1901, courtesy New York State Library, 14. Courtesy Library of Congress, Detroit Publishing Company Collection, 17. Don Barbeau, 19, 21. Jim Shaughnessy, 20. Albany *Times-Union,* 24. Courtesy Fleet/Norstar Financial Group, 27, 39. Morris Gerber, 63. Francis Poulin, 86. The Photographers & Co., for Light & Power Productions, 91.

Front cover photo by Howard J. Wolff for Einhorn Yaffee Prescott PC. Photo of the author by Donna Abbott. Architectural drawings on cover, title page, and page 11, courtesy of The Houghton Library, Harvard University, Department of Printing and Graphic Arts.